BOYS
IN THE
REVOLUTION

BOYS IN THE

Young Americans tell their part

WITH DRAWINGS AND CONTINUITY

Stackpole Books

REVOLUTION

in the War for Independence

BY JACK COGGINS

Harrisburg, Pennsylvania

CONTENTS

ABOUT BOYS
in the Revolution

THE HISTORY OF the Revolutionary War is full of accounts of the deeds of the officers and enlisted men who fought so gallantly for American freedom. Yet there is little mention of the part—an important part—played by the boys— some of them only ten or twelve years old. Some of them enlisted and fought in the ranks or served aboard ship. The adventures of three such youngsters are told in this book. There were many others, though, whose stories have gone unrecorded, boys who braved danger ashore and afloat. Besides these, there were others, who, by shouldering the responsibilities of grown men, released a father or elder brother to join Washington's little army.

Fortunately for America, her wars of the last 100 years have all been fought overseas. It is hard to imagine the effect on the people of Colonial times of a war which raged up and down the countryside for so many years, a war in which Americans fought not only the British, Hessians, and Indians, but other Americans as well. Danger was on everyone's doorstep in those days. The tramp of marching feet might mean the arrival of the redcoats, or the thudding of hooves at night, a raiding party of Tories. In the outlying settlements many a family fled to the comparative safety of a nearby log fort, while their houses and barns flared redly behind them, and the woods echoed with the dreaded war whoop.

So war often came to boys too young to shoulder a musket with the soldiers of the Continental Army. It was a war in which the enemy had no way of knowing which Americans were friendly, merely indifferent, or hostile.

In such a war, an intelligent boy was often of great service to the American side. By hanging around British camps or in towns where troops were quartered, he picked up valuable information. A boy could do this without arousing suspicion, whereas the presence of a grownup would be distrusted at once. As taproom boys or waiters in taverns and inns, they might overhear scraps of conversation about the enemy's troop movements or the location of military stores and supplies.

In an enemy camp, there were many ways in which a patriot boy could make himself useful. He could run errands for officers, fetch water or firewood, work as cook's helper and handy boy, and bring in supplies, such as eggs, milk, butter, and vegetables, from his family's and neighbors' farms. Many a redcoat fell in ambush because of a careless word spoken within hearing of a sharp-eared boy.

Boys knew the local countryside better, perhaps, than anyone and many times acted as guides for American forces. On the other hand, British troops who relied on a smart young patriot found themselves hopelessly lost in a maze of strange woods or bogged down in swamps.

In territory occupied by the enemy there was a well-organized underground. A clever boy made a perfect messenger and often delivered or received messages right under the very noses of the British without their suspecting him. A "printer's devil," or errand boy in a printing office, frequently delivered or distributed anti-British pamphlets. These served to raise the morale of the patriots and to annoy their enemies.

There were various means of harassing the British. A tarpaulin split by a boy's sharp knife could let in rain enough to spoil a whole wagonload of flour. A hole drilled in a barrel could spill a flood of rum or a dangerous trickle of gunpowder. It was difficult to sabotage a wagon, but by slashing the horses' harness a supply line could be stalled for some time.

While the war waged on land, an equally fierce struggle went on at sea. The Continental Navy was very small, but in every port, merchantmen were

7

fitted out with armament to attack British commerce. With the addition of a few small cannon and swivel guns, a fishing vessel could easily be turned into an armed raider. These craft preyed upon British shipping with great boldness and captured cargo vessels under the very bowsprits of the Royal Navy's ships.

All vessels, even the smallest coaster, employed one or two boys. They were cook's helpers, cabin and ship's boys, and, in the Navy, powder boys commonly called "powder monkeys," and "loblolly" boys. These last were the boys who served the loblolly, or thick gruel prescribed by the surgeon for sailors in sick bay. "Loblolly" is also a nautical slang word for medicine and, actually, the loblolly boys were doctor's helpers.

Some boys went as apprentice seamen. They would be called cadets today. These were often the sons or relatives of sea captains or ship owners and were sent aboard with the idea of learning the rudiments of navigation and ship-handling. But it was a hard service. At a time when, in the Royal Navy, a ship's rat was often considered a delicacy by His Britannic Majesty's midshipmen, the life of even an apprentice in a merchant ship was a miserable one. Many a shivering youngster with wet clothes and an empty belly cried himself to sleep in a swaying hammock or creaking bunk. And he often nursed ribs bruised from a knotted rope's end wielded by some irate mate or bos'n, for discipline was severe to the point of being brutal.

In a modern warship, ammunition is supplied to the guns by machinery, but in Washington's day the powder had to be fetched by hand from the magazines or storerooms deep in the ship's hold. This duty was performed by boys, powder monkeys.

Their job was to receive the bags of powder from the gunner's mate in the hold, rush up the ladders with them to the decks where the guns were flashing and roaring, and hand the bags to the loaders. The gun deck of a ship in action was a terrible place, dark with choking powder smoke, swept by showers of deadly splinters of wood and the iron hail from the enemy's guns. Despite the sand which had been sprinkled around before the ship went into action, the decks soon became slippery with blood. And the panting powder monkeys often stumbled over the bodies of their shipmates. It was dangerous work, but it was not often that a gun was silenced for lack of ammunition, and then usually because the faithful boy supplying it was dead or wounded. Someone has called the boys who fed powder to American naval guns, the forgotten heroes of the Revolutionary War.

Boys ashore fought too, whenever necessary. Most American boys were taught to shoot at an early age. The land was wild and undeveloped for the most part and a short walk from the center of even the largest colonial town brought one into open country or forest. There was game in plenty. Almost every family owned some sort of firearm and many sons not in their teens became as good shots as their fathers. When war came, they were able to take their place in a skirmish with the enemy, along with the men.

The average Colonial used only the smoothbore musket, which was wildly inaccurate at anything over 100 yards. Some of the frontiersmen, however, carried the far deadlier rifle known as the "Kentucky rifle," which was really developed and made in Pennsylvania. This weapon was accurate enough for a good shot to pick off game or hit a target at 200 yards or more. The owning of a Kentucky rifle was the dream of every frontier boy.

The British had suffered badly from the expert marksmanship of the Americans as early as the first pitched battle of the Revolution, the Battle of Bunker Hill, where the loss of men was so great all England was shocked.

Back in London, a man hearing the news of the British victory with over a thousand officers and men killed or wounded, cried, "We're victorious! If we have eight more such victories there'll not be a soldier left alive to bring back the report!"

The American—man or boy—had learned by experience that he could not afford to waste so much as a single shot. Many times a farm boy, or plow-jogger, as he was sometimes contemptuously called, had had to depend upon one shot to bring down a meal—a goose or other game—and he dared not miss, or he and his family would go hungry. He knew his gun and, in using it, took into account its particular crankiness. When he fired at something, he expected to hit it.

This was not true of the British or Hessian soldier. He had been trained to fight in a line with other soldiers. At the command, "Fire!" the whole line fired a volley. The soldiers aimed in the general direction of the target, expecting that out of many shots some were bound to hit the enemy. When soldiers in the line were killed or wounded, the rest closed ranks and on command fired another volley.

Two years after Bunker Hill, on October 16, 1777, at the Battle of Saratoga, the British commanded by General John Burgoyne, who had helped win the costly Bunker Hill victory, suffered one of the great defeats of the war. America's expert marksmen, some of them only fourteen or fifteen years old, played their part.

The three boys of this book, John Greenwood, Ebenezer Fox, and Joseph Martin, all recorded what they did in the war. John Greenwood began his account with events that took place in Boston when he was a small boy, some years before the outbreak of war. He was only eight years old in 1768 when British soldiers landed at Long Wharf. These troops were being stationed in Boston as a police force to help King George's officials enforce the unpopular tax laws. Before John was seventeen he was to help drive those soldiers out, campaign in Canada, and take part in Washington's great victory at Trenton.

The war had not yet begun that spring of 1775 when twelve-year-old Ebenezer Fox, disgusted with the harsh life of a farmer's helper, ran away to sea. From Providence, Rhode Island, he made his

9

first voyage, as cabin boy in a West India-man. Fighting broke out while he was at sea, and by the time the war was over Ebenezer had fought in a savage naval battle, been imprisoned in a dreadful floating jail, and made a thrilling escape from a tropical island.

Joseph Martin was fifteen, the same as John Greenwood, when war broke out in 1775. He lived with his grandparents on their farm near Becket, a village in Massachusetts, not far from the New York boundary line. He was too young to enlist as a fighting man, and so was among those left behind when the men and older boys quit their farms to go to war. When he did enlist, in June 1776, the British had evacuated Boston but were about to attack New York. Joseph wore the blue coat of a Continental

soldier for seven long years, and saw men of Washington's command change from a poorly armed mob to a disci-plined army of veterans. He saw, too, the final scene where, to the tune of "The World Turned Upside Down," Corn-wallis' red-coated regiments marched out of their battered entrenchments at York-town to lay down their arms.

Between them, the three boys saw battle in many forms—Indian fighting in the North Woods, the shattering broadsides of a naval engagement, and the volleys and bayonet charges of regu-lar warfare. Like many American boys, they did their duty. Unlike most others, though, they wrote about their adven-tures, and it is from their accounts that the following stories are written.

CHRONOLOGY
of the War of the Revolution

1775

April 19 • Battles of Lexington and Concord. War begins.
May 10 • Ethan Allen and his Green Mountain Boys of Vermont capture Fort Ticonderoga.
Second Continental Congress assembles.
June 12 • First naval battle. At Machias, Maine, lumberjack Jeremiah O'Brien and local partisans seize British naval cutter "Margaretta."
June • **Ebenezer Fox, a cabin boy on a West Indiaman, escapes capture by British by diving over side.**

June 15	•	Congress elects George Washington to command the Continental Army.
June 17	•	Battle of Bunker Hill.
June 17	•	**John Greenwood with his regiment, the Twelfth Massachusetts, is stationed near Bunker Hill.**
July 3	•	General George Washington takes command of American forces at Cambridge, Massachusetts, and siege of Boston begins.
September 1	•	General Richard Montgomery leaves Fort Ticonderoga with force to capture Montreal, Canada.
September 17	•	Colonel Benedict Arnold leaves Boston with force to push through Maine forests to capture Quebec, Canada.
November 12	•	Montreal falls to General Montgomery.
December 3	•	First Lieutenant John Paul Jones hoists the flag of freedom (the "Jack and Stripes") aboard flagship "Alfred" of the first American Navy of eight ships in Delaware River at Philadelphia.
December 31	•	Forces of Montgomery and Arnold unite in assault on Quebec. Montomery killed. Arnold lays siege to city.

1776

March	•	British evacuate Boston. Washington moves his army to New York.
April 21	•	**John Greenwood's regiment sails up Hudson to Albany on way to Montreal, Canada.**
May 6	•	Arrival of British fleet in St. Lawrence River forces Americans to withdraw from Quebec.
June 1	•	**Joseph Martin enlists in the Massachusetts troops.**
June 15	•	**John Greenwood leaves Montreal with remnants of the Twelfth Massachusetts.**
June 28	•	British forces under General Sir Henry Clinton and Lord Cornwallis make unsuccessful attack on fort at Charleston, South Carolina.
July 2	•	Congress adopts resolution declaring the Colonies independent of Great Britain.
July 4	•	Declaration of Independence proclaimed.
July 2- August 12	•	General William Howe lands with several thousand troops on Staten Island, New York. His brother, Admiral Lord Richard Howe, arrives with battle fleet, men and supplies.
August 26	•	British under General Howe defeat Americans under General Washington at Battle of Long Island.
August 27	•	**Joseph Martin and Massachusetts regiment arrive at Gowanus Creek after American defeat in Battle of Long Island.**
November 20- December 8	•	After series of defeats, Washington and his army retreat across New Jersey.
December 25	•	Washington crosses the Delaware.

December 26	•	Hessian troops (German mercenaries) surrender to Washington at Battle of Trenton.
December 26	•	**John Greenwood's Twelfth Massachusetts takes part in the battle.**
December 27	•	**John Greenwood, his enlistment up, starts back home to Boston.**

1777

January 3	•	Washington defeats British at Princeton, New Jersey, and goes into winter quarters at Morristown.
April 12	•	**Joseph Martin re-enlists, this time in Eighth Connecticut Regiment, which later in spring engages in skirmishes with British near Danbury, Connecticut.**
July 1	•	General John Burgoyne begins siege of Fort Ticonderoga.
July 6	•	Americans evacuate Ticonderoga.
August 16	•	General John Stark defeats Colonel Frederick Baum and Hessians at Battle of Bennington, Vermont.
September 11	•	Howe defeats Washington at Battle of Brandywine.
September 26	•	Philadelphia falls to Lord Cornwallis.
October 17	•	General Horatio Gates, reinforced by Colonel Daniel Morgan's Rifle Corps, checkmates British attempt to occupy Hudson River-Lake Champlain Valley and cut Colonies in two by defeating General Burgoyne at Battle of Saratoga.
November	•	**Joseph Martin's Eighth Connecticut, on guard duty near New York City, is marched to Pennsylvania, then ordered to forts on Delaware River, which British force it to abandon.**
November 15	•	Congress presents the Articles of Confederation for ratification by the thirteen states.
December 15	•	Washington with his army goes into winter quarters at Valley Forge, Pennsylvania.

1778

February 6	•	France and American Colonies sign treaty of commerce and alliance.
April 22	•	Flying new flag, the "Stars and Stripes," Captain John Paul Jones in war-sloop "Ranger" raids English seaport of Whitehaven.
May	•	George Rogers Clark with force of volunteers sets out from Williamsburg, Virginia, on expedition against British forts on Wabash, Ohio, and Mississippi rivers.
June 18	•	General Sir Henry Clinton evacuates Philadelphia.
June 28	•	Washington wins Battle of Monmouth Courthouse, and Clinton retreats to Sandy Hook.
June 28	•	**Joseph Martin is a participant in the battle.**

August 12	•	French fleet under Comte d'Estaing puts to sea from Narragansett Bay to fight British fleet under Admiral Howe. Both fleets scattered and damaged by great storm.
November 11	•	Settlements raided and farms destroyed by Tories and Indians in Cherry Valley Massacre.
December 29	•	French and Americans defeated by British fleet and troops at Savannah, Georgia, and city falls.

1779

February	•	**Ebenezer Fox signs on the naval ship "Protector."**
February 23-24	•	Clark completes successful expedition to Northwest by capturing Vincennes.
May 10	•	British expedition from New York burns Portsmouth and Norfolk, Virginia.
May 30	•	Clinton sails up Hudson, captures Stony Point and King's Ferry.
June	•	Spain joins France in support of the Americans.
June 18	•	General John Sullivan begins expedition against Six Nations, Indian allies of British.
July 15	•	General Anthony Wayne recaptures Stony Point from British, destroys, then abandons fortifications.
August 29	•	Sullivan defeats British regulars, Tories and Indians at Newtown, New York (now Newtown Battlefield Reservation park).
August	•	**Ebenezer Fox is aboard "Protector" when she engages in battle with British Admiral Duff.**
September 12	•	Comte d'Estaing arrives from West Indies with French troops and lands them at Savannah, Georgia. French and Americans lay siege to city.
September 23	•	Captain John Paul Jones in "Bonhomme Richard" captures H.M.S. "Serapis" off Flamborough Head on east coast of England.
October 9	•	Siege of Savannah fails. Americans retire to Charleston. French troops re-embark.
December	•	**Ebenezer Fox, captured by British in naval encounter, is sent to prison ship "Jersey," moored off Long Island shore.**
December 26	•	Clinton and Cornwallis sail from New York for Charleston, South Carolina.

1780

March 29 .	•	British under Clinton and Cornwallis begin siege of Charleston.
May 12	•	Charleston surrenders.

July 10- July 21	•	French fleet arrives at Newport, Rhode Island, with troops under Comte de Rochambeau and is blockaded by British fleet.
Summer	•	**Joseph Martin is promoted to sergeant in newly formed Corps of Sappers and Miners.**
August 16	•	Americans under Gates defeated by Cornwallis at Camden, South Carolina.
September 23	•	General Benedict Arnold's plot to surrender West Point to British discovered.
October 2	•	Execution of Major John André as British spy at Tappan, New York.
October 7	•	Mounted frontier riflemen defeat British under Colonel Patrick Ferguson at King's Mountain, North Carolina.

1781

January	•	**Joseph Martin in barracks at West Point, New York. With coming of spring, scouting parties engage in skirmishes with Tories.**
January 17	•	Colonel Banastre Tarleton is defeated by Americans under General Daniel Morgan at Cowpens, South Carolina.
August 22	•	Cornwallis withdraws his entire British force to Yorktown, Virginia.
August 25	•	Washington and Rochambeau with the combined American and French armies start for Yorktown from the Hudson River.
August 25	•	**Joseph Martin and the Corps of Sappers and Miners are first to set out for Yorktown.**
August 30	•	Comte de Grasse with French fleet and troop transports from West Indies arrives in Chesapeake Bay.
September 5	•	British fleet commanded by Admiral Thomas Graves arrives at mouth of Chesapeake. In naval battle, French force British to withdraw.
September 10	•	Comte de Barras arrives from Newport, Rhode Island, with French siege artillery. De Grasse bottles up mouth of York River.
September 30	•	Americans and French begin siege of Yorktown held by British under Cornwallis.
September 30	•	**Joseph Martin and his corps arrive at Yorktown.**
October 5	•	**Joseph Martin and sappers help engineers with laying out and digging trenches in preparation for assault on British defense works and forts.**
October 19	•	Cornwallis surrenders at Yorktown and afterward, British army begins its evacuation of Savannah, Charleston and New York.
October 19	•	**Joseph Martin as a soldier in the Continental Army is present at ceremony of the surrender of Cornwallis and his army.**

1783

Spring • **Ebenezer Fox, seaman on American ship "Flora," which is laid up in Bordeaux, France, because of British blockade, serves until after signing of peace treaty.**

September 3 • Treaty of Paris. Compact formally ends the War of the Revolution.

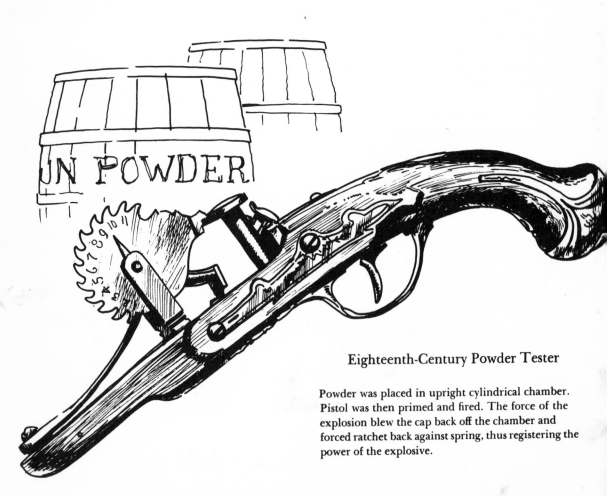

Eighteenth-Century Powder Tester

Powder was placed in upright cylindrical chamber. Pistol was then primed and fired. The force of the explosion blew the cap back off the chamber and forced ratchet back against spring, thus registering the power of the explosive.

JOHN GREENWOOD
and his Fife

IN THE SPRING OF 1775, the eastern sea-board of North America was in turmoil. The long-smoldering resentment of the colonists against the government in London had burst into flame on a village green at a place called Lexington. Now the land was on fire, from the rocky harbors of Maine to the swamps of the Carolinas. Everywhere companies of militia were being formed and men were drilling, while blacksmiths, gunsmiths and all makers of weapons and munitions worked to arm and equip the forces of the revolution.

The seat of the trouble and the scene of many acts of violence before the actual beginning of the war was the city of Boston. Here in May, 1760, was born John Greenwood, whose bold spirit was one day to lead him into some strange adventures.

Bright uniforms and the sound of martial music took young John's fancy early. When very young, he was taken for a walk by a Negro boy belonging to the family. Entranced by the drums and fifes of a company of British soldiers, John followed them until he was too tired to go any farther. The Negro boy took him into a shop to rest and ran on after the soldiers, forgetting where he left his charge. The result was that Johnny's parents had to call for the Town Crier, the colonial combination of newscaster, advertising man, and lost-and-found department.

Throughout the streets of Boston, the man went crying, "Little boy lost. His name is John Greenwood, son of. . . ." until young Johnny was found.

Later young John learned to play the fife himself, and, as he said: "Trifling as it may seem to mention the circumstance, it was, I believe, the sole cause of my travels and disasters.

"I was so fond of hearing the fife and drum played by the British that somehow or other I got possession of an old split fife," he recalled. "Having made it sound by puttying up the crack, I

learned to play several tunes upon it sufficiently well to be fifer in the militia company of Captain Gay. This was before the war some years, for I think I must have been about nine or ten years old. The flag of the company was English. So were they all then."

Boston was an exciting place in those days. John's father was an ivory turner, a craftsman who shaped articles of ivory on a lathe. His apprentice and John's good friend, Sam Maverick, was one of the five killed in the so-called Boston Massacre of March 5, 1770. This occurred when a squad of exasperated British soldiers, set upon by a stone-throwing mob, fired a volley into the crowd. John

was not present at that affair although his twelve-year-old brother was.

"But," said John, "I saw the tea when it was destroyed at Boston, which began the disturbance, and beheld several persons tarred and feathered and carried through the town."

When he was thirteen, John was sent to live with his uncle in the little seaport of Falmouth, Maine. There he was soon playing his fife for his uncle's company of militia.

He had, "as it were, imbibed the ardor of a military spirit; being moreover the only boy who knew how to play the fife in the place."

News of the fighting at Lexington and

Concord on April 19, 1775, soon reached Falmouth. Worried by the wild tales of fighting, plundering, and burning in and around Boston, John decided it was time to set out for home.

"My reason for going," he wrote in his reminiscences, "was that I wished to see my parents who, I was afraid, would all be killed by the British, for nothing was talked of but murder and war."

He knew that his uncle would not permit a boy just turned fifteen to make a long journey of 150 miles alone on foot. So, one Sunday morning when he was not likely to be missed, John took a handkerchief and tied up in it two or three shirts and a pair or two of stockings. "And, with what clothes I had on my back and four-and-a-half pistoreens in my pocket, I jumped over the fence in the backyard and set off." Pistoreens were Spanish coins used in the West Indies at the time and worth at most twenty-five cents each.

He also had a sword, perhaps one of those issued to his uncle's company of militia. But, most important of all, John had his fife.

His journey took him through some lonely and rough country, but he made good time, better than thirty miles a day. He made friends all the way from Falmouth, Maine, to Boston, Massachusetts, and paid for his board and lodging with his fifeplaying.

"Stopping at taverns where there was a muster (a calling together of the militia), out came my fife and I played them a tune or two," he related. "They used to ask me where I came from and where I was going to. When I told them I was going home to fight for my country, they were astonished that such a little boy, and alone, should have such courage. Thus by my fife I lived, as it were, on what is usually called free-quarters nearly upon the entire route."

He finally arrived at Charlestown, across the river from Boston. But the Americans would not allow him to go any farther. The British had already been penned up inside the city and the siege of Boston was beginning. After spending a few days with the American army, which was not yet a regular, organized military force, John enlisted for eight months as fifer in Captain Bliss's company of the Twelfth Massachusetts Bay Regiment of Foot, commanded by Colonel John Patterson.

On the morning of June 17, John's regiment was stationed within sight of Bunker Hill. Although it took no part in the battle, John remembered seeing the wounded brought down from the battlefield. The road leading from Bunker Hill was "filled with chairs and wagons, bearing the wounded and dead." The chairs John referred to were sedan chairs, enclosed seats slung between two poles.

"Groups of men were employed in

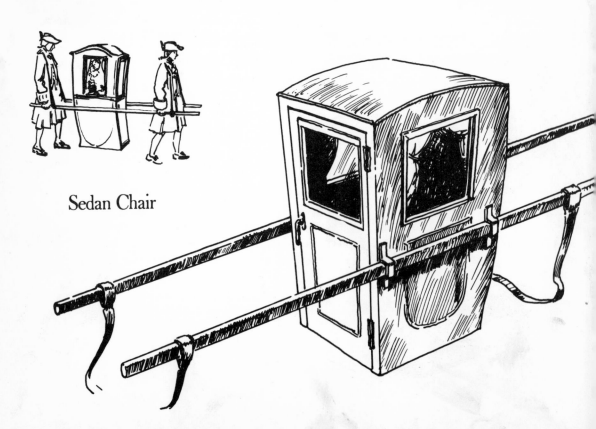

Sedan Chair

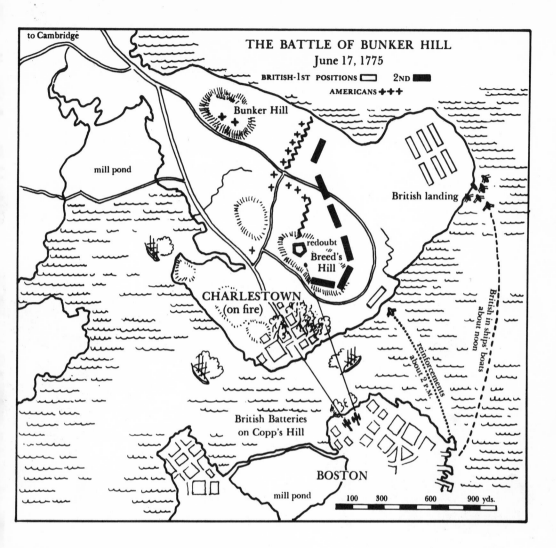

THE BATTLE OF BUNKER HILL
June 17, 1775

BRITISH-1st POSITIONS ▭ 2ND ▬
AMERICANS +++

to Cambridge

Bunker Hill

mill pond

British landing

redoubt
Breed's
Hill

CHARLESTOWN
(on fire)

British in ships' boats
about noon

reinforcements
about 2 P.M.

British Batteries
on Copp's Hill

BOSTON

mill pond

100   300   600   900 yds.

assisting others, not badly injured, to walk," he recalled. "Never having beheld such a sight before, I felt very much frightened and would have given the world if I had not enlisted as a soldier."

The battle itself was brought on by the decision of the Colonials to fortify Bunker Hill, a high point on one of the small peninsulas which make up Boston Harbor. On the night of June 16,

some 1,100 men under Colonel William Prescott secretly crossed Charlestown Neck, which joined the little peninsula to the mainland. Whether by accident or design, no one knows, the line for the entrenchments was laid out on a lower hill, called Breed's Hill. As quietly as possible, so as not to alarm the British patrol boats, the farmers who made up the force plied mattock and spade.

Dawn found them still laboring, and

the works—a small earth-walled fort, or redoubt, and a breastwork—were completed amidst the shriek of round shot from the British ships and the incessant roar of their broadsides, as well as the long-range fire of howitzers and mortars from a battery on Copp's Hill in Boston.

Except for a few lucky hits little damage was done, but it was sufficient to cause many of the militia to drop their tools and run. Across the harbor in Boston, drums beat and church bells rang as British General Thomas Gage called his troops to arms.

Any fortification of the heights surrounding the city threatened the British garrison, and preparations were made to attack the rebel works at once. Unfortunately for the British they made the mistake of waiting until high tide allowed the boats landing the troops to pull right up to the beach. This six-hour delay gave the Americans time to finish their works and prepare for the attack.

As the redcoats moved in ordered ranks toward the entrenchments on Breed's Hill, the patriots pressed the stocks of their muskets against their cheeks and waited. The cannonade stopped as the red lines began to climb the slope. Slowly, stumbling in the tall grass and over low stone walls, bumping into wooden fences, sweating under their heavy packs, the British regulars pushed up the hill closer to the American lines. When only fifty yards away, they met a blaze of musketfire that mowed them down. Of those in the companies that advanced to turn the American left flank, ninety-six lay dead when they finally broke and ran.

The tall grenadiers in the center fared no better. General William Howe led the attack against the breastworks, and every man of his personal staff was either killed or wounded. As the firing continued, the second line came up, but served only to increase the slaughter. Finally the whole array fell back in confusion.

But the battle was not over. Fifteen minutes later, the British had straightened their shattered ranks and were again moving forward.

"An incessant stream of fire poured from the rebel lines. It seemed a continued sheet of fire for nearly thirty minutes," wrote a British officer who was in the battle.

Grenadier's Cap

And once more the survivors rolled back down the slope. Some of the companies had lost nine-tenths of their men, but once more the British began to reform their ranks.

While the British reorganized, the American leaders tried to persuade some of the hundreds watching the struggle to come to the aid of their comrades, who were by now desperately short of ammunition. On Bunker Hill, not more than 600 yards away, many hundreds of fresh troops were standing. Yet none moved to the battle. Down the slope the drums were beating and once more the redcoats were advancing, reinforced now by 400 fresh men and a column formed from the boat-guards and all the wounded who could walk.

Again the British were met by a heavy fire, but this time they could not be stopped. As they leaped the ditch and climbed the parapet the fire of the defenders slackened. Some of the Colonials were bayoneted where they stood, others were shot as they fled from the gate or in the retreat. The retreat itself was orderly, covered by the musketry of some new arrivals from the mainland. So ended the celebrated Battle of Bunker Hill.

Technically it was a British victory, but they had paid a heavy price for it. Out of some 2,400 men, including the reinforcements, 226 were killed and 828 wounded. The American losses were about 140 killed, 271 wounded, and 30 captured. Although they lost their earthworks, they had the satisfaction of knowing that they had beaten back in disorder some of the finest infantry in the world.

. British Infantry — Privates of Line and *(right)* Grenadier Companies

Despite the loss of Bunker Hill, the Americans held Boston in an ever tightening grip. On July 2, 1775, General George Washington had arrived at Cambridge to take command of the Continental Army. The loosely organized rebel military force began to take on the shape and discipline of a real army. Soon after Washington's arrival there was, an observer noted, "a great overturning in the camp as to order and regularity. The strictest government is taking place and great distinction is made between officers and soldiers. Everyone is made to take his place and keep it."

Colonel Patterson's regiment was part of this growing Continental Army. Fifer Greenwood's account mentioned several skirmishes as the besiegers drew closer and closer around the city.

"The British were constantly sending bombs at us," he wrote. "And sometimes from two to six at a time could be seen in the air overhead, looking like moving stars in the heavens. These shells were mostly thirteen inches in diameter and it was astonishing how high they could send such heavy things. I have often seen them strike the ground when it was frozen and bound up like a football and, again falling on marshy land, they would bury themselves from ten to twelve feet in it. Whereupon, the wet ground having extinguished the fuses, the Yankees would dig them up to get the powder out."

"On one occasion," John remembered, "a 13-inch bomb dropped directly opposite the door of the picket guardhouse where two hundred men were on duty. A lad about eighteen years old, named Shubael Rament, belonging to our company, ran out, knocked the fuse from the shell, and took the powder out of it, of which I had some myself to kill snipe with."

HEAVY MORTAR

Shell, sponge and
tongs for carrying shell

Floating Battery

John also mentioned the floating batteries with which the Americans planned to batter down the British defenses. As shown in a drawing of the time, these were strongly built scows, with thick planking, having openings for long oars just above the waterline and loopholes above them for muskets. At each end of the floating battery was a gunport for a cannon. On the deck there were four swivels, small cannon fastened on forklike mounts which turned in sockets. These could be easily turned in any direction and were often used in small vessels to beat off attacks by boarders.

The town of Charlestown, on the same peninsula as Bunker Hill, had been set on fire during the battle and almost destroyed. The few houses left standing were used as shelters by some of the British. One winter night, 200 Americans, many carrying bundles of chips soaked in turpentine, crossed the narrow neck of land and approached the houses.

Greenwood, now a fife-major, went along more for the adventure than anything else, for the march had to be made in strictest silence up to within a few dozen yards of the British sentries and one peep out of a fife would have brought disaster. As it happened, all went well. Some prisoners were taken and the houses set afire "right under their very noses, the enemy at the fort being so astonished as not to fire for some time, at least not until the houses were in a light blaze. I never heard that we lost a single man," Greenwood said.

The long winter passed with a few such minor actions. The chief worry of the troops was the lack of firewood. All the fences and trees for miles around were cut down. As General Washington wrote in a letter, "Different regiments were upon the point of cutting each others' throats for a few standing locusts."

But what concerned Washington and

27

his officers far more than the scarcity of wood was the lack of arms and, even more serious, the difficulty of holding the army together. Desertions were common. In addition, few men agreed to remain in the army after their enlistment periods were up. They went back to their farms and homes by the hundreds, nor could orders, pleas, or promises prevent them.

"Such a dirty, mercenary spirit pervades the whole," wrote their disgusted Commander-in-Chief, "that I should not be at all surprised at any disaster that may happen."

However, some hardy souls, among them Fife-Major John Greenwood, re-enlisted and others came in to volunteer.

Small quantities of arms and ammunition became available. By almost superhuman feats of strength and endurance, General Henry Knox's men dragged, hauled, and floated the artillery captured at Fort Ticonderoga across lakes, rivers, and mountains to the Americans besieging Boston. Thus strengthened, Washington decided to attempt to break the deadlock. The British, unable to afford another costly victory such as Breed's Hill, could not get out of the city. On the other hand, the Americans were not strong enough to make an assault upon it.

On the night of March 4, Washington made his move. Dorchester Heights was seized and fortified under cover of darkness.

"At the latter work we went," goes Greenwood's account, ". . . . and having all the fascines ready made, the British were in the morning surprised at beholding a fort which would have so great a command over them." Fascines were long bundles of branches of trees used in constructing earthworks or embankments.

Whether John took his turn with pick and shovel or encouraged the workers with his fife, he did not say. In any event, the hastily built entrenchments so dominated the Boston harbor that it was obvious to the British that they would have to evacuate the city. But before they finally embarked on March 17, 1776, John's regiment had begun a move to another theater of war, one where they would face hardship, hostile Indians, hunger and disease; and from which many would not return.

28

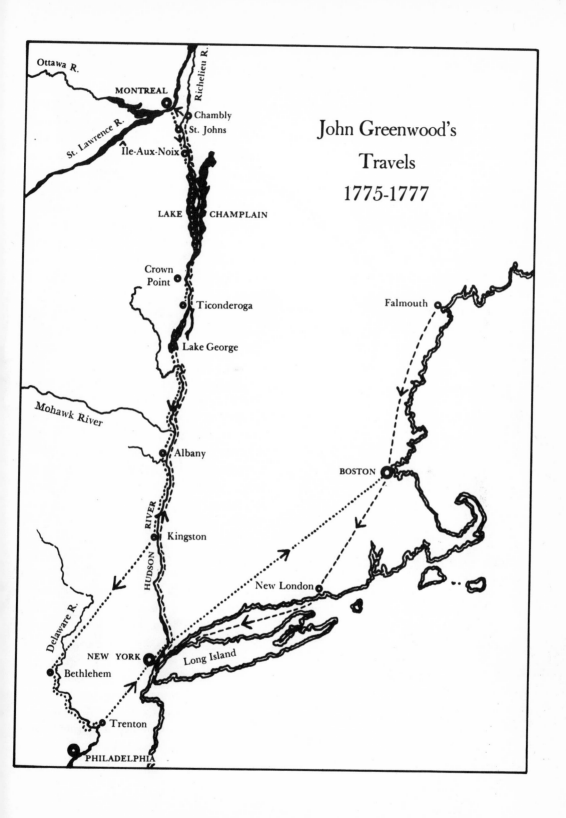

Ottawa R.

MONTREAL

Richelieu R.

Chambly

St. Johns

St. Lawrence R.

Île-Aux-Noix

LAKE   CHAMPLAIN

John Greenwood's

Travels

1775-1777

Crown
Point

Ticonderoga

Falmouth

Lake George

Mohawk River

Albany

BOSTON

HUDSON   RIVER

Kingston

New London

Delaware R.

Long Island

NEW   YORK

Bethlehem

Trenton

PHILADELPHIA

Virginia Rifleman   Continental Dragoon

With drums banging and fifes shrilling, the Twelfth Massachusetts marched to New London, Connecticut, where the regiment embarked for New York. On April 21, it sailed from that city up the Hudson River to Albany on the first leg of the journey to Montreal, Canada.

The journey was evidently an uneventful one. John dismissed it in his account with a line or two.

Of the troops he wrote, "Our regiment consisted at the time of 500 strong and tolerably well-disciplined soldiers, badly equipped as to guns, however, as the majority of them had fowling-pieces of different sizes and bores and few of them had bayonets. Moreover, the men were unfurnished with swords to fight with in close quarters, although a few of them had tomahawks."

A greater threat than actual combat was smallpox. The Massachusetts men had not been in Montreal many days before a number of them had contracted the disease and were hospitalized.

Soon after John Greenwood's arrival in Montreal, a force of about four hundred Americans was attacked by a small body of English and Canadians, accompanied by some five hundred Indian allies. The Americans surrendered without putting up much of a fight, and a reinforcement of two hundred men on the way to help them was ambushed and captured. General Benedict Arnold at once collected another force of men, among them John Greenwood, and led them against the Indians.

A scout, a deserter from the British Rangers, was sent ahead and John was chosen to accompany him. John was not

Powder Horn

too happy about his companion. "I never liked a deserter or a traitor, neither can be trusted," he said.

However, the two reached a farmhouse about eight miles from Montreal without incident. They were no sooner inside than they heard the fearful war whoop. In a few minutes, the house was surrounded by Indians. John and the scout crawled under a big bed. It was a terrible moment.

"Had they found us we would have been burned alive," John said.

Although redmen swarmed around the house, the Canadian farmer and his Indian wife did not betray John and the scout. And, in a little while, the Indians, who were retreating before Arnold's advance, left.

The two scouts now set off in pursuit. They discovered that the band was on its way beyond the St. Lawrence River, crossing it near St. Anne. John and his companion returned to General Arnold with the information, John limping most of the way, having injured his foot in jumping over a fence.

John related what happened then: "The troops were soon mustered for pursuit. As I could not walk without much pain, I was obliged now to get into one of the boats. The river being very rapid, it was late before these bateaux or boats got up to Fort Anne and the sun was about two hours' high. The troops were in readiness to embark and follow the enemy, so on board they came. I had the command of a blunderbuss at the bow of our boat. General Arnold was in a birch canoe, paddled by two Indians who belonged to a party of two hundred that had joined us after our arrival at La Chine, opposite to which place they have

32

a town called Caughnawaga."

As the American force neared the bank, muskets flashed and banged along the edge of the forest, and two small brass cannon opened fire on the crowded boats.

". . . . which made our Indians fly with their birch canoes like so many devils," said Greenwood. "They do not like to see large balls skipping over the water, in and out until their force is lost, for a single one would knock their paper boats to pieces in a moment."

Arnold wisely ordered a retirement to the other bank, where many fires were lighted to give the impression of a much larger force than was actually present. In the morning, under a flag of truce, an exchange of prisoners was arranged with the enemy. The men captured in the American defeats were then returned and Arnold and his troops went back to Montreal.

Although there were supposedly 8,000

33

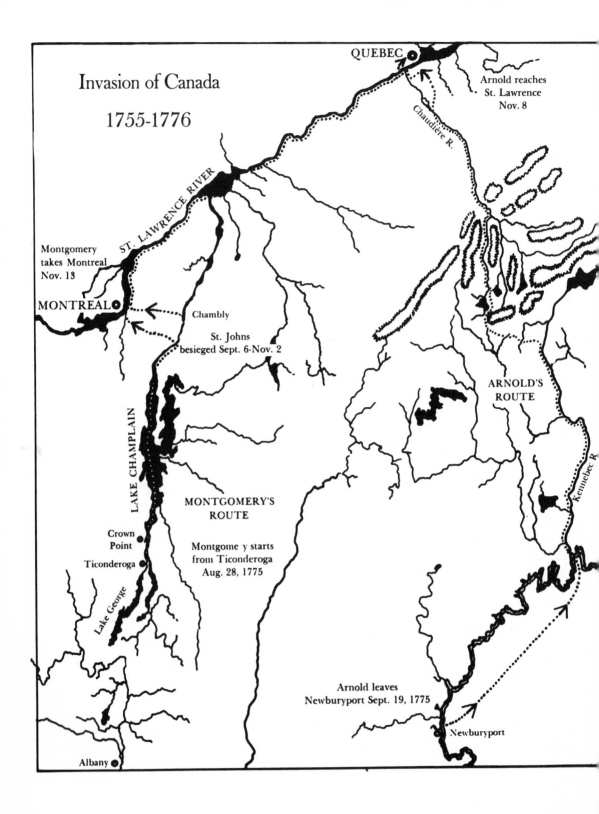

Invasion of Canada

1755-1776

QUEBEC

Arnold reaches
St. Lawrence
Nov. 8

Chaudière R.

ST. LAWRENCE RIVER

Montgomery
takes Montreal
Nov. 13

MONTREAL

Chambly

St. Johns
besieged Sept. 6-Nov. 2

ARNOLD'S
ROUTE

Kennebec R.

LAKE CHAMPLAIN

MONTGOMERY'S
ROUTE

Crown
Point

Montgome y starts
from Ticonderoga
Aug. 28, 1775

Ticonderoga

Lake George

Arnold leaves
Newburyport Sept. 19, 1775

Newburyport

Albany

Americans in the Lake Champlain-St. Lawrence River region, many of them were sick and others weak from fatigue and insufficient food. A shortage of trained physicians and a complete lack of sanitation and hygiene, of which there was little knowledge in those days, made life in camp almost as deadly as on the battlefield.

By now all hope of taking Quebec had been abandoned by the Americans. A force under General John Burgoyne, consisting of eight British regiments and 2,000 German mercenaries had arrived in the St. Lawrence. The American troops besieging Quebec went back up the river in great haste and disorder. When 6,000 Colonials arrived as reinforcements, the American commander might have turned the tide. But a defeat at Trois Rivières, about halfway between Montreal and Quebec, on June 8, 1776, decided the issue. Retreat was the only course left, and the long, agonizing journey back to Crown Point, at the southern end of Lake Champlain began.

What was left of John Greenwood's Twelfth Massachusetts Regiment was in Montreal when General Arnold ordered the town abandoned on June 15, and the troops embarked in haste not much ahead of the advancing British.

"Down we scampered to the boats, those of the sick who were not led from the hospital, crawling after us," wrote Greenwood. "Camp equipage, kettles, and everything were abandoned in the utmost confusion, even the bread that was baking in the ovens, for we were glad to get away with whole skins. When halfway across the river, it began to grow very dark, and down came the rain in drops the size of large peas, wetting our smallpox fellows, huddled together like cordwood in the boats, and causing the death of many."

After reaching shore, the bedraggled army was rounded up and marched off through mud "half a leg deep" in the direction of La Prairie. Next day the march was resumed. The sick and wounded were placed in vehicles, carts and wagons which the officers commandeered from the neighboring farmers.

The whole force was collected at St. Johns (or Fort St. John) on the Richelieu River at the northern end of Lake Champlain. The troops then set off in boats for the island, Île-aux-Noix, a few miles up the river. On this low, swampy island, about a mile long and a quarter of a mile wide, some 8,000 men disembarked. Over 2,000 of them were sick with smallpox. Within a couple of days another 1,500 were down with malaria or dysentery. Black flies and mosquitoes swarmed in clouds over sick and well alike.

Firewood was scarce, although that seemed of small importance, since there was nothing to cook but a little rancid salt pork and flour. Medicine gave out and the dead were heaped in common graves. To stay at Île-aux-Noix meant the complete destruction of the army, so the men piled into their boats once more, the half-sick rowing the helpless and dying, and went down the lake to Crown Point.

John Greenwood had little to say about this part of his adventures. Perhaps they were too terrible for him even

Iroquois Warrior with War Club and
Musket. *Above:* wooden mask of
False Face Society. *Below:* quiver,
stone axe, and trade hatchet.

Bateaux, Such as Were Used in Arnold's March to Quebec

to try to recall. He did mention that his rations on the way down the lake were a pint of flour and a quarter of a pound of salt pork per day.

They landed each day at noon to cook this sumptuous repast, without any cooking utensils. The flour was mixed with water from the lake, and the dough was "made and baked upon a piece of bark, so black with dirt and smoke, I do not think a dog could eat it," John said.

Since he was a bit small to ply an oar, he cheered his fellow boatmen with tunes on his fife.

From Crown Point, they went to Ticonderoga where the remnants of Patterson's and of other New England regiments were encamped on Mount Independence.

Greenwood recalled that it was "covered with thick woods and, being also very rocky, was filled with snakes of every description, though mostly black and rattlesnakes."

The winter was setting in. Toward the end of November, orders came for the Twelfth Massachusetts to join Wash-

ington's army in New Jersey. Because of the bad weather, poor food, and the constant exposure to wet and cold, many men were sick. Of the 500 men who had set out for Canada that spring of 1776, only 100 were left. Even young Greenwood was now sick, and the march to Albany was a terrible one.

"With no tents to shelter us from the snow and rain," he wrote, "we are obliged to get through it as best we can. And, as to eating and cooking, you may put them out of the question."

From Albany, they sailed down to Kingston, "and thence proceeded, still without tents, and some of our men without even shoes, over the mountains to a place called Newtown, in Pennsylvania, passing on the way through Nazareth and Bethlehem." Thus, in a few lines, the fifer passed over what must have been a long, harsh and painful march. It would have been a rough journey for men in the best of condition. Many of the starving, shivering men died before they reached the Delaware River.

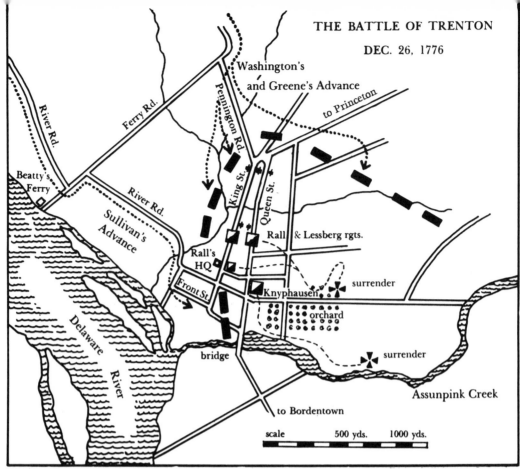

Washington's
and Greene's Advance

to Princeton

River Rd.

Ferry Rd.

Pennington Rd.

King St.

Queen St.

Beatty's
Ferry

River Rd.

Sullivan's
Advance

Rall & Lessberg rgts.

Rall's
HQ

surrender

Front St.

Knyphausen

orchard

Delaware

River

surrender

bridge

Assunpink Creek

to Bordentown

scale   500 yds.   1000 yds.

At the end of 1776, Washington's forces of a few thousand men had retreated from New Jersey and were on the Pennsylvania side of the Delaware while the British, under Howe, were strung out in winter quarters across New Jersey.

Washington was in desperate need of a victory. The enlistments of many of his gambling, hungry, half-clad troops expired on December 31. He wanted, if possible, to check a threatened British march on Philadelphia before his army dispersed. Also, a victory might induce many men to re-enlist as well as cheer up those who remained. Washington's troops were too few to defend the river successfully against a surprise advance

by the British. He therefore decided that the best defense was an attack. He made plans for a concentrated assault on Trenton, New Jersey, in which three columns of men would cross the Delaware at different places and converge on the town at daybreak.

The enemy's troops quartered in Trenton were, with the exception of a troop of dragoons, all Germans. There were three regiments of Hessians, 1,400 of them, with six field pieces. Washington knew that Christmas Eve and Christmas Day would be celebrated in hearty German fashion, with much feasting and drinking. Accordingly, he ordered the attack for first light on December 26, when the garrison could be expected to be sleeping off their holiday festivities.

The men of the Twelfth Massachusetts were part of the main column under General Washington himself, with General Nathanael Greene and General John Sullivan as corps commanders. As the troops began the march to their crossing places, a storm broke, which grew in intensity as the night wore on and the time for attack drew closer.

John Greenwood described what happened in these words: "If I recollect aright, the sun was about half-an-hour high and shining brightly, but it had no sooner set than it began to drizzle and grow wet. When we came to the river it rained. Every man had sixty rounds of cartridges served out to him. As I then had a gun, as indeed every officer had, I put the number which I received, some in my pockets and some in my little cartridge box.

"Over the river we then went in a flat-bottomed scow and, as I was with the first that crossed, we had to wait for the rest. So we began to pull down the fences and make fires to warm ourselves, for the storm was increasing rapidly.

"After a while it rained, hailed, snowed, and froze. At the same time, it blew a perfect hurricane, so much so that I perfectly recollect, after putting the rails on to burn, the wind and the fire would cut them in two in a moment and, when I turned my face toward the fire, my back would be freezing."

The storm hid the advance of the troops and muffled the clashing of their accoutrements and the rumbling of the artillery wheels.

Dragoon Private, Brunswick

Colonel Johann Rall, leader of one of the Hessian regiments and commanding officer in Trenton, had been warned of the attack by a Tory. That is, the man had tried to warn the colonel. The story goes that a messenger rode to the house where Rall was being entertained and demanded to see him. Refused admittance, the messenger wrote a note informing Rall that the Americans were marching toward Trenton. He gave the note to a servant, telling him to deliver it at once. But cards and wine were on the colonel's mind that night and he slipped the note unread into his pocket. It was found on his body after the battle.

The surprise was complete. Emerging from a curtain of sleet and snow, the American columns, striking from three sides, overran the outlying guardhouses and their dazed occupants.

As the Hessian drums beat out the alarm, the Americans swiftly advanced into the town. Cannon were placed to rake the streets and, as the bewildered Germans poured out of their billets and formed outside, their ranks were torn by grape- and round shot. The Hessians wheeled their guns into position, but the American riflemen, stationed in various houses, picked off the gun crews before they could fire more than a few

40

times. Attempts by the Germans to reform and charge were met by blasts of cannonfire and the crackle of musketry. Although gunlocks had been carefully wrapped in greased cloth, rain had got in and wet the powder in the pans, disabling many muskets. As a result, much of the fighting was hand-to-hand with sword and bayonet.

It was a wild scene, with flashes from the guns bright under the dark sky, lighting up the snow flurries and making the bayonets gleam. Everywhere there was confusion. Bodies lay thick underfoot in the slush and mud. And, above the yells and cheers of the fighting men, could be heard the screams of the wounded.

Young John was in the thick of it. "The first intimation I received of our going to fight," he recalled, "was the firing of a 6-pound cannon at us, the ball from which struck the fore horse that was dragging our only piece of artillery, a 3-pounder. The animal, which was near me as I was in the second division on the left, was struck in its belly and knocked over on its back. While it lay there kicking, the cannon was stopped and I did not see it again after we passed on.

"As we advanced, it being dark and stormy so that we could not see very far ahead, we got within two hundred yards of about three or four hundred Hessians who were paraded, two deep in a straight line, with Colonel Rall, their commander, on horseback, to the right of them. They made a full fire at us, but I did not see that they killed anyone. Our brave Major Sherburne ordered us to fall back about three hundred yards and pull off our packs, which we accordingly did and piled them by the roadside.

" 'Now, my boys,' says he, 'pass the word through the ranks that he who is afraid to follow me, let him stay behind and take care of the packs!'

"Not a man offered to leave the ranks and, as we never went back that way, we all lost our packs. At least, I never heard anything of mine and I had in it a beautiful suit of blue clothes, turned up with white and silver laced."

John went on to tell what took place after that: "As we had been in the storm all night, we were not only wet through and through ourselves, but our guns and powder were also wet. I do not be-lieve one would go off and I saw none fired by our party. When we were all ready, we advanced. Although there was not more than one bayonet to five men, orders were given to 'Charge bayonets and rush on!' and rush on we did.

"Within pistol shot they again fired point blank at us. We dodged and they did not hit a man. Before they had time to reload, we were within three feet of them, when they broke in an instant and ran like so many frightened devils into the town which was at a short distance, and we after them pell-mell.

"Some of the Hessians took refuge in a church at the door of which we stationed a guard to keep them in. And, taking no further care of them for the present, we advanced to find more, for many had run down into the cellars of the houses.

"I passed two of the cannon, brass 6-pounders, by the side of which lay seven dead Hessians and a brass drum. This latter article was, I remember, a great curiosity to me and I stopped to look at it. But it was quickly taken possession of by one of our drummers who threw away his own instrument. At the same time, I obtained a sword from one of the bodies and we then ran on to join the regiment, which was marching down the main street toward the market.

"Just before we reached this building, however, General Washington, on horseback and alone, came to our major and said, 'March on, my brave fellows, after me!' and rode off."

Colonel Rall was killed trying to rally his men. The rest of his regiment was surrounded and forced to surrender. An

42

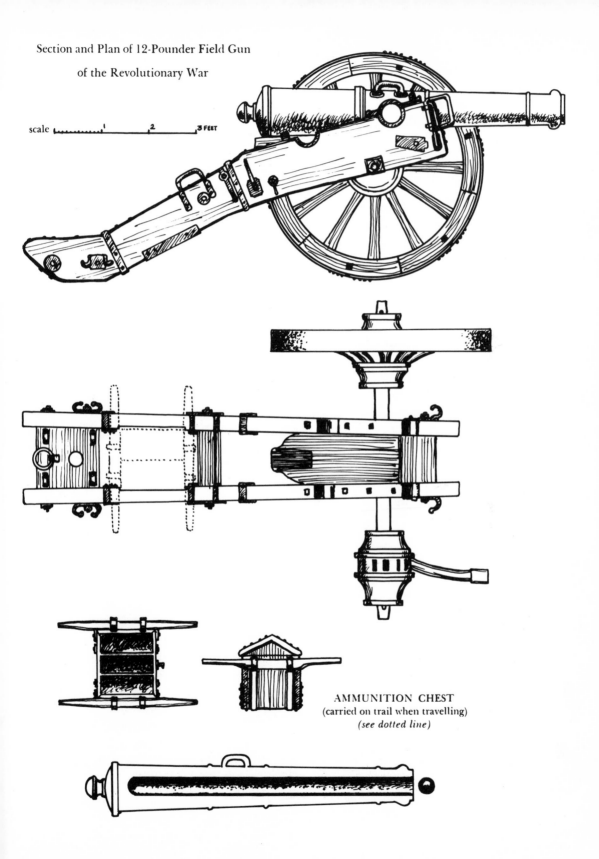

Section and Plan of 12-Pounder Field Gun
of the Revolutionary War

scale |⎯⎯⎯⎯1⎯⎯⎯⎯2⎯⎯⎯⎯3 FEET

AMMUNITION CHEST
(carried on trail when travelling)
(see dotted line)

attempt by the two other Hessian regiments to break out of the trap failed. The bridge across the Assunpink Creek was too strongly held. Attempts to find a ford failed and their two cannon bogged down in a swamp. Surrounded by American troops and with men falling fast, the Hessians lowered their colors. The men laid down their muskets and the officers raised their hats on their swords' points in surrender. Trenton was won. Washington had his victory.

There were 948 prisoners taken, with six field pieces, wagons, horses, and fifteen regimental and company colors. John's regiment was set to rounding up prisoners and captured weapons.

Brass Cap of Hessian Fusilier

"A number of wagons came behind us," Greenwood wrote, "into which the guns were placed. The next thing we were ordered to disarm the prisoners of their swords, with one of which every man was provided. These we also put in the wagons, but compelled the enemy to carry their cartridge boxes themselves. Our regiment was then ordered to conduct the prisoners down to the ferry and transport them over to the other side. So, we began the march, guarding the flanks or sides of the roads."

The prisoners, or at least some of them, were grenadiers. They had been told that the Americans were cannibals who would skin poor German soldiers to make drumheads and feast on their roasted carcasses.

"On the march down to the boats, seeing some of our men were much pleased with the brass caps which they had taken from the dead Hessians, our prisoners, who were exceedingly frightened, pulled off those that they were wearing and gave them away. Then they put on the hats which they carried tied behind their packs. With these brass caps on, it was laughable to see how our soldiers would strut—fellows with their elbows out and some without a collar to their half-a-shirt, no shoes, etc."

John's time had been up the day before the battle. On December 27, 1776, the day after the battle, he received three months' back pay. "And glad was I," he said.

Although he was offered a promotion to ensign, he was tired and ill and wanted to go home.

"I told him [his company lieutenant]

I would not stay to be a colonel. I had the itch then so bad that my breeches stuck to my thighs, all the skin being off. There were hundreds of vermin on me, owing to a whole month's march and having been obliged for the sake of keeping warm to lie down at night among the soldiers who were huddled close together like hogs."

With another young fifer, Greenwood started out on the long walk home.

"We were both sick," he later wrote, "and I from weakness could hardly put one foot before the other. Yet we trudged along together, with one blanket, expecting to reach Boston, the route we had to take being about 350 miles."

He had thirty-three paper dollars in his pocket. His pay as fife-major had

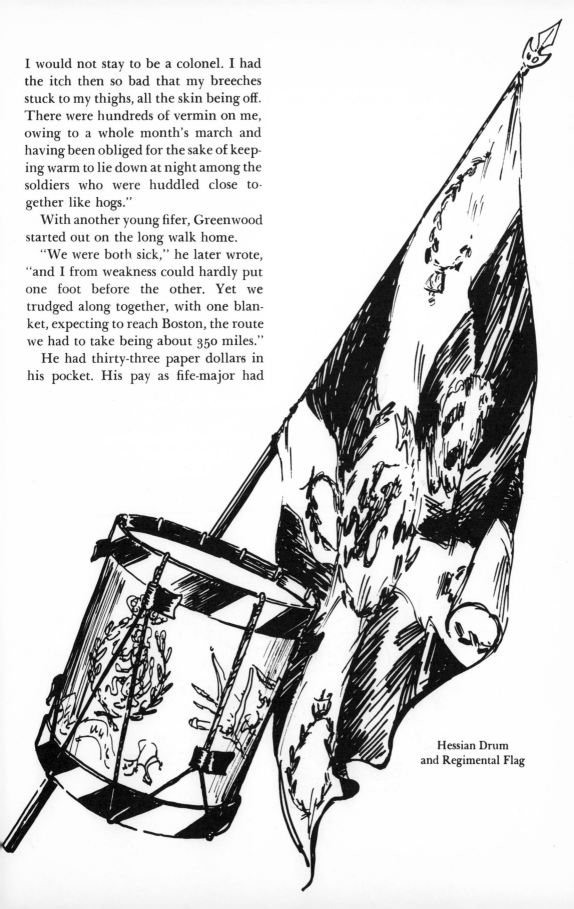

Hessian Drum
and Regimental Flag

been eleven dollars a month. With eleven dollars, he bought a horse. He then had to bargain with a farmer at a nearby house for a saddle, for "riding him without one was out of the question." Not only were the legs of both fifers sore and inflamed from the itch, but the horse's back was "as sharp as a knife." The saddle was an old one, with two loops of rope for stirrups and another piece of rope for a bridle. The whole thing cost two dollars.

They rode the animal, which John likened to Don Quixote's Rosinante for boniness, "tie and tie."

"That is, I would ride it two miles and, tying it in the road, walk on. When Parks [his companion] came up, he would mount and overtake me. In this way, we kept on three or four days when, at last, poor Parks gave out and could go no further."

John rode on alone (who kept the single blanket, he did not say), occasionally sleeping next to the fireside of some hospitable country folk. Finally, he reached King's Ferry on the Hudson River. Here ferry traffic was halted for several days because of the ice in the river.

"At last, it parted in such a way as to leave an opening for the ferryboat to venture across," John wrote. "The boat had four or five horses in it, besides being filled with passengers. We just got across in time to jump out, for a large cake of ice, near half-a-mile long, coming down with the tide, struck the boat and carried it some distance down the river. Some of the horses, I recollect, were then in her, but whether I got mine out or not I have forgotten.

"This much I do remember, however, that I travelled home on foot from the east side of the North River. When I arrived at my father's house in Boston, the first thing done was to bake my clothes [in the oven to destroy the vermin] and then to anoint me all over with brimstone [sulphur]."

Eighteenth Century Saddle

EBENEZER FOX,
the Sailing Barber

JOHN GREENWOOD'S TRAVELS took him to Canada. The adventures of Ebenezer Fox led him to the tropical island of Jamaica and, finally, to France.

Ebenezer was born in Roxbury, Massachusetts, in 1763. His father, a tailor, was a poor man with a large family. In those days it was customary, when parents had more children than they could support, to place one or more of them in homes where the boys and girls worked for their keep. Thus, at the age of seven, Ebenezer was sent to live with a farmer's family.

He lived with them for five years, doing chores and working in the fields. But it was a hard life, with many beatings, and finally he rebelled. With his possessions in a bundle on his back and all his money, half a dollar, in his pocket, Ebenezer ran away. In company of a friend of his own age, he set out for Providence, Rhode Island. They traveled part of the way by stagecoach, paying a small fare for their seats on the baggage, which was carried over the rear axle.

Providence, in the spring of 1775, was a busy port. In a few months, as the British blockade tightened, the busy wharves would be silent, and the rope walks, where hemp was fashioned into cordage, would be shut down, while the ships rotted at anchor. But when the two boys arrived, Turner's Wharf and the other docks and piers were crowded with shipping, while vessels of all sizes, from coasters to whalers and lofty Indiamen, swung at their moorings in the harbor.

In Providence, the friends parted. Twelve-year-old Ebenezer, after roaming the docks for a few days looking for work, signed on a merchantman as cabin boy. His pay was twenty-one shillings a month, or about four dollars, which was half that paid a seaman.

The ship was bound with merchandise for the West Indies. The Americans, particularly the New Englanders, carried on a thriving trade with the

islanders. They sold salt pork, fish and beef, hides, flour, lumber and other products there, and brought back sugar, usually a dark, moist unrefined cane sugar called muscovado, and molasses, rum, green turtles, pimientos, salt from Turks Island, coconuts, sponges and dye-woods.

Like many landlubbers on their first days at sea, Ebenezer was seasick. But, once recovered, he soon learned his duties of helping the cook, waiting on table at the officers' mess and running errands.

The ship reached the island of Hispaniola and anchored at Cap Français (present-day Cap Haitien). There she took on a cargo of molasses and sailed for home.

In the meantime, war between the

49

American colonies and the mother country had broken out, and British warships had begun a blockade of American ports. Between Newport and Providence, Rhode Island, the vessel was trapped by British men-of-war. To escape capture, the captain ran his ship aground and the crew, including Ebenezer, dived over the side.

"I plunged into the sea and swam ashore," he related in his account of his experiences. "I arrived without injury, but nearly exhausted with fatigue and fear, not a little augmented by the sound of the bullets that whistled around my head while I was in the water."

Fearing pursuit, Ebenezer stripped off his wet clothes and ran for it. He arrived naked at a farmhouse, where a friendly farmer lent him some clothes.

One might think that such an end to his first voyage would have soured Ebenezer on a sailor's life. Far from it. Four days later, in his borrowed clothes, the boy sailed again for Cap Français. This voyage was completed without incident, in spite of the fact that the Americans had to run the gauntlet of British warships all the way there and back. With his four dollars in wages in his pocket, Ebenezer went proudly home to Roxbury to visit his parents.

Deciding to learn a trade, Ebenezer became apprenticed to a barber. His principal work, he wrote, "was in the preparation of hair for the purposes of wigs. Occasionally, I was allowed to scrape the face of a transient customer who might be reasonably expected never to call again for a repetition of the operation."

For almost four years he worked at learning his trade, but he found shaving faces and making wigs pretty dull work after his experiences at sea. A brief escape from the barber shop soon came. The barber, a member of the Roxbury militia, found to his dismay that he had been drafted to serve in the reinforcement that was being sent to the American army near New York. In those days, a draftee was permited to hire a substitute, provided, of course, that he had enough money. This the unhappy barber could not afford to do, but he prevailed upon his young apprentice to serve in his place. So Ebenezer shouldered a musket and set off for the wars.

His military service consisted of acting as convoy guard to a wagon train of ammunition. His memory of it, like that of so many soldiers, was chiefly of sore feet and an empty stomach. Of valiant deeds there were none. But Ebenezer did remember that a stolen goose was successfully hidden in a drum, and a raid on an uncharitable farmer's henhouse netted him and his companions three dozen chickens.

When, after three months, the emergency was over, Ebenezer and the rest of the militia were discharged, left to get home as best they could.

Ebenezer stayed with his barber for a few more months, but the urge to go to sea again grew too strong. At last, with his employer's consent, but on the conditions that he receive half Ebenezer's wages and half any prize money he might win, young Fox signed on the "Protector," a state government ship of twenty guns.

G R E A T
ENCOURAGEMENT
F O R
SEAMEN.

ALL GENTLEMEN SEAMEN and able-bodied LANDSMEN who have a Mind to diftinguifh themfelves in the GLORIOUS CAUSE of their Country, and make their Fortunes, an Opportunity now offers on board the Ship RANGER, of Twenty Guns, (for France) now laying in Portsmouth, in the State of New-Hampshire, commanded by JOHN PAUL JONES Efq; let them repair to the Ship's Rendezvous in Portsmouth, or at the Sign of Commodore Manley, in Salem, where they will be kindly entertained, and receive the greateft Encouragement.---The Ship Ranger, in the Opinion of every Perfon who has feen her is looked upon to be one of the beft Cruizers in America.---She will be always able to Fight her Guns under a moft excellent Cover; and no Veffel yet built was ever calculated for failing fafter, and making good Weather.

Any Gentlemen Volunteers who have a Mind to take an agreable Voyage in this pleafant Seafon of the Year, may, by entering on board the above Ship Ranger, meet with every Civility they can poffibly expect, and for a further Encouragement depend on the firft Opportunity being embraced to reward each one agreable to his Merit.

All reafonable Travelling Expences will be allowed, and the Advance-Money be paid on their Appearance on Board.

IN CONGRESS, MARCH 29, 1777.

RESOLVED,

THAT the Marine Committee be authorifed to advance to every able Seaman, that enters into the Continental Service, any Sum not exceeding FORTY DOLLARS, and to every ordinary Seaman or Landfman, any Sum not exceeding TWENTY DOLLARS, to be deducted from their future Prize Money.

By Order of Congress,
JOHN HANCOCK, President.

DANVERS: Printed by E Russell, at the Houfe late the Bell-Tavern.

Recruiting for the Continental Navy was usually done by parties of smartly dressed sailors headed by a jovial, smooth-talking officer. On a street corner or in the town square, an American flag would be set up. Sometimes the flag was the "rattlesnake flag" with "Don't tread on me" printed on it. Other times, it was the "Jack and Stripes." The beating of a drum or the swinging of a dinner bell by one of the sailors attracted attention.

When a crowd had gathered, the officer would shout through a leather speaking trumpet: "Hear ye. Hear ye. All able-bodied seamen and patriotic Americans." Then he would give the name of the ship and when she was expected to sail and wind up by asking for enlistments. Usually there were promises of a bonus at the end of the war besides, perhaps, fifty acres of land.

CUTAWAY DRAWING OF A TYPICAL

Warships of two hundred years ago were comparatively small. The one below measures only some 160 feet on the upper deck which was perhaps 40-feet at its widest. From the quarterdeck to the bottom of the hold measured about 30 feet. Into this space were crammed some 500 men with food (such as it was) and water to supply them for a voyage which might last several months. Each ship was a self-contained unit and carried, besides her guns, powder and shot, spare timber for the ship's carpenters, iron for her blacksmiths, rope cordage and cloth for her sailmakers and riggers and even firewood for the cooks.

The space at the stern (9) and (11) below, was reserved for the officers. It was divided into tiny cabins by partitions of thin wood or canvas which were removed when the ship was cleared for action. The

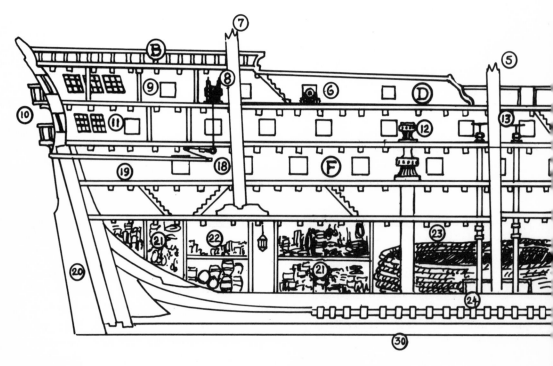

A. Forecastle Deck
B. Poop Deck
C. Forecastle
D. Quarter Deck
E. Upper Deck
F. Lower Deck
G. Orlop Deck
H. Hold

1. Figure head
2. Bowsprit
3. Fore Mast
4. Hammock Rail
5. Main Mast
6. Gun Port
7. Mizzen Mast
8. Wheel
9. Upper cabin
10. Stern galleries

captain (and admiral if the vessel was a flagship) occupied the best spaces in the stern, but even these were cramped, and the highest ranking officers often shared their quarters with a couple of heavy cannon. The lesser officers occupied even more undesirable quarters on the lower deck (19) and the petty officers slung their hammocks on the orlop deck (G). The cockpit (27) was usually reserved for the midshipmen and the wooden chests which held their belongings were often used as operating tables, for this space was the ship's surgery when in action.

The seamen and marines slung their hammocks on the lower deck, fourteen inches to a man. Headroom on the gun decks was less than six feet between the beams, and on the orlop deck less than that. A sailor's life in those days was no picnic.

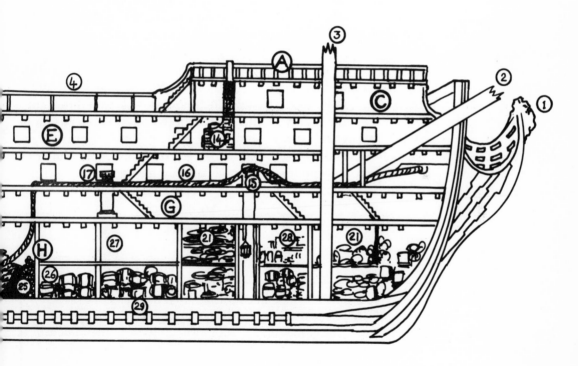

11. Lower cabins	21. Stores
12. Main capstan	22. After Magazine
13. Pumps	23. Cable Tier
14. Galley	24. Pump Well
15. Bitts	25. Shot Lockers
16. Cable	26. Water casks
17. Forward capstan	27. Cockpit
18. Tiller	28. Forward Magazine
19. Warrant officer's quarters	29. Keelson
20. Rudder	30. Keel

Also, one suspects that enlistments were encouraged by liberal portions of free rum. At any rate, by the time the "Protector" was ready to put to sea, many of her crew had evidently regretted their joining the Navy.

"Upwards of three hundred and thirty men," wrote Ebenezer, "were carried, dragged and driven aboard, of all kinds, ages, and descriptions, in all the various stages of intoxication. Such a motley group had never been seen since Falstaff's ragged regiment paraded the streets of Coventry." Ebenezer referred to Sir John Falstaff, the fat jovial, rascally knight who was comrade to the Prince of Wales in Shakespeare's play, *King Henry IV.*

Fortunately, the officers of the "Protector" had time to whip their unpromising collection of recruits into some sort of shape before they met the enemy.

After cruising the New England coast and the Grand Banks for several weeks, the lookouts sighted a large ship under English colors, bearing down on them.

Captain Williams, commanding the "Protector," decided to give battle.

Young Fox described the preparation for the encounter: "The shrill pipe of the boatswain summoned all hands to their duty. The bedding and hammocks of the sailors were brought up from between decks. The bedding was placed in the hammocks and lashed up in the nettings.

"Our courses [sails on the lower yards] were hauled up and the topgallant sails clewed down. Every preparation was made which a skillful officer could suggest or active sailors perform."

The gun crews ran to their stations while marksmen took their places in the tops. Boys sanded the decks, while others, the powder monkeys, ran to the magazine for cartridges. The wooden plugs, called tampions, which were fitted into the muzzles of the guns to keep out spray and damp, were removed, the cartridges pushed down the bores, and the iron cannon balls rammed down on top. The gun ports were hauled up and the loaded

Naval guns were cast of iron. They were rated according to the weight of the ball they threw: 3-, 6-, 9-, 12-, 18-, 24- and 32-pounders. The carriages were of wood, with wooden wheels (trucks). The gun was cast with two projections (trunnions), which rested in two semi-circular depressions in the top of the carriage and were held in place by hinged caps.

The gun was elevated by levering the breech up with handspikes, and sliding a wooden wedge (quoin) under it. Recoil was checked by a heavy rope (breeching) which ran through a ring lashed to the breech and was fastened to the ship's side. Tackle was used to run the gun up to the gun port for firing, to pull it back, and to help train it from side to side. Handspikes were also used to train the gun.

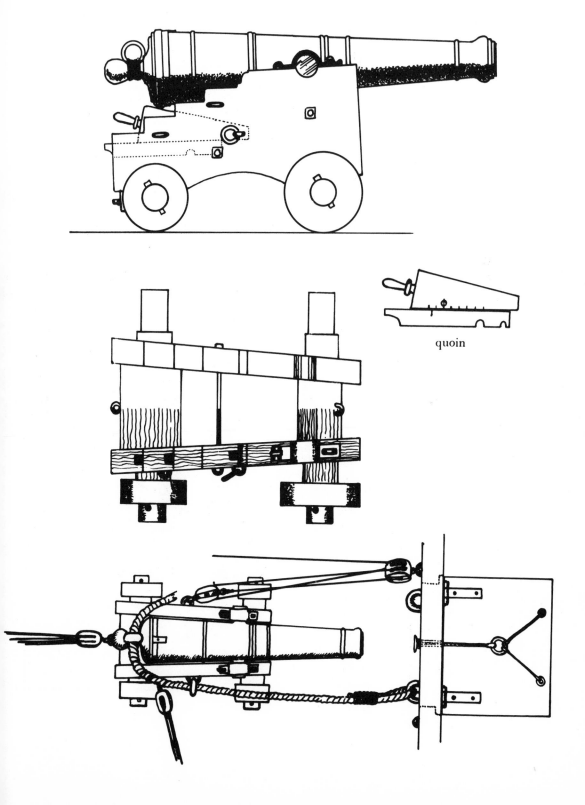

quoin

guns run out. Fuses of cotton wicking soaked in lye or some such substance, called slow matches, were lighted and placed in tubs of sand between the guns. They were used to fire the cannons. Fire buckets were filled. The carpenter and his mates prepared to plug any shot holes below the water line, while the surgeon and his assistants laid out bandages and instruments in the cockpit.

To deceive the enemy until the last moment and to give the "Protector" a ·chance to escape if the British ship proved to be a man-of-war, the American vessel flew British colors.

The enemy was hailed, and proved to be the "Admiral Duff," thirty-two guns, bound for London from St. Kitt's. The English captain hailed in his turn. Finding that five guns would bear on the Britisher, the American captain in reply ordered the flags to be shifted and fire commenced. "The cannons poured forth their deadly contents and, with the first flash, the American flag took the place of the British ensign at our masthead."

The fight was a fierce one. Ebenezer was one of the gun crew of a six-pounder. His job was to swab out the gun after each discharge, then ram down the powder and ball. Dense smoke, lit by the glare of the guns, soon covered the vessels. Broadsides crashed out as fast as the sweating gun crews could load.

Deadly wood splinters flew through the air as round shot crashed into the ship's sides. Amid the howl of the shot and the screams of the wounded, young Ebenezer swabbed and rammed, swabbed and rammed until the gun

56

grew hot. The "Protector's" fire was well aimed and made a terrible slaughter among the enemy crew. Although the ships were within close range, the American losses were light.

A shot by one of the company of marines aboard the "Protector" killed the British helmsman. The "Admiral Duff" sheered in, with her bowsprit over the "Protector's" forecastle. Thinking that the British were about to board, the Americans seized cutlasses and boarding pikes and prepared to drive them off. However, the British quickly cut their rigging away and drew clear.

and mizzen tops of the enemy. The action had now lasted about an hour and a half. The fire from the enemy had begun to slacken when we suddenly discovered that all the sails on her mainmast were enveloped in a blaze. The fire spread with amazing rapidity and, running down the after-rigging, it soon communicated with her magazine and her whole stern was blown off and her valuable cargo emptied into the sea."

American Naval Officer

Again the broadsides crashed out. As Captain Williams paced back and forth on the quarterdeck, a shot struck the speaking trumpet from his hand, but he calmly picked it up and resumed his pacing.

"The battle," Ebenezer recalled, "still continued with unabated vigor on both sides, till our marksmen had killed or wounded all the men in the fore, main,

Seaman

Now, all efforts were made to rescue the burned and wounded survivors, struggling in the water. The "Protector's" boats had been damaged, but repairs were quickly made and fifty-five men were picked up.

Ebenezer came through his first naval battle without a scratch, although serving his gun for an hour and a half had made him partially deaf.

Repairs were made, mostly to the vessel's rigging. Since the British had fired high, few shots had struck the hull, and the "Protector" resumed her cruise. When provisions ran short, she made for Boston, which she reached after

being chased by a British frigate. Had the "Admiral Duff" been taken instead of destroyed, her sale would have brought the "Protector's" crew a large sum in prize money. As it was, Ebenezer Fox landed in Boston little richer than he started out.

Hoping his luck would change, Ebenezer signed up for a second cruise. For a while all went well. Several vessels were taken and a prize crew put aboard each of them, to sail the captured ships to American ports. For this purpose, the "Protector" carried a very large crew, far more men and officers than were needed to handle the ship.

Prison Hulk "Jersey"

One unlucky day, the lookout reported, "Two sails to leeward." They proved to be British frigates, one of forty guns and the other of twenty-eight. Swifter as well as more heavily armed than the "Protector," they were soon alongside. An eighteen-pound shot across the American's bow warned her to heave-to. Resistance was hopeless. The American flag came flapping down and a British boarding party swarmed over the rail and took possession. The "Protector's" cruise was at an end.

The next few months were the most terrible of Ebenezer's life. In an age when all prisoners could expect to be treated badly, the British prison hulks were notorious. The worst of them all was the "Jersey" to which Ebenezer and his shipmates were sent on their arrival in New York.

Nicknamed "The Hell Afloat," the "Jersey" was an old seventy-four-gun vessel which was too decayed to be sea-worthy. She had been stripped of her armament and masts and converted into a prison ship. She had been originally moored in the East River, "but in consequence of the fears that were entertained that the sickness, which prevailed among the prisoners, might spread to the shore, she was removed," Ebenezer wrote. "She was moored with chain cables at the Wallabout, a lonely and unfrequented place on the shore of Long Island, not far from Brooklyn. Her external appearance was forbidding and gloomy. She was dismantled, her only spars were the bowsprit, a derrick that looked like a gallows, for hoisting supplies on board; and a flag staff at the stern. The portholes were closed and secured. Two tiers of holes were cut through her sides, about two feet square and about ten feet apart, and strongly guarded by a grating of iron bars."

Hustled aboard, Ebenezer found there were over 1,000 prisoners there already. "They were covered with rags and filth; visages pallid with disease, emaciated with hunger and anxiety, and retaining hardly a trace of their original appearance. They were shriveled by a scanty and unwholesome diet, ghastly with inhaling an impure atmosphere, exposed to contagion, in contact with disease, and surrounded with the horrors of sickness and death."

The food, scanty though it was, probably was not much worse than that issued to the wretched seamen of the British fleet. But overcrowding, lack of hygiene, medical attention, and sanitary facilities, and, after a while, despair of ever escaping alive, all combined to take a terrible toll of the inmates. Hundreds died and were buried in the mud flats off which the grim hulk was moored.

In spite of the guards, escapes were made from time to time. The prisoners were allowed on deck during the day and herded below at sunset. One evening, Ebenezer and several fellow prisoners managed to hide themselves in a closet in the forecastle. Hardly daring to breathe, they huddled in their cramped quarters while the rest of the prisoners were locked between decks. When darkness came, there was a good chance, Ebenezer and the others thought, that they could slip overboard unseen. Unfortunately, an oversuspicious mate decided to search the ship thoroughly, including the closet.

Just as he opened the door, the Americans dashed out. Swinging cutlasses and clubs, the guards closed in on them. There was a brief struggle, during which a guard slashed Ebenezer in the side with a cutlass. The prisoners were quickly overpowered and chained hand and foot. They were left lying on deck where they spent a cold, rainy night. As further punishment, their already meagre rations were cut by one-third for a month.

Cutlass and Sheath

Some of the healthier prisoners were conscripted for service in the Royal Navy. Others were induced by threats and promises to enlist in British regiments stationed abroad, on condition that they would not be called upon to fight their own countrymen.

In despair of escaping the horrors of the "Jersey," with its daily toll of patriots dead from disease and malnutrition, Ebenezer at last consented to join the service as a private in a British regiment stationed in Jamaica. He hated to sign the papers which made him a soldier of King George III. But, besides promises of food, clothing, and easy duty in the garrison, there was always the chance of deserting and finding a way home. The great difficulties of escaping from an enemy-held island over 1,400 miles away, not to speak of the risk of hanging for the crime of desertion, might have daunted many a man, but not Ebenezer Fox. His one idea was to get home somehow.

The regiment to which he was assigned was stationed in Kingston. Other than long hours of drilling in the barracks' square and the task of keeping his weapons and accoutrements in good order, there was little to do except plot escape.

Ebenezer's skill as a barber was soon discovered and he became barber and hairdresser to the officers of the regiment. This not only relieved him of most of his duties as a common soldier, but also brought him into the good graces of his superiors, a fact which was to be of great importance.

With five companions, whose special skills had won them privileges similar to his own, Ebenezer began to plot how to escape from the island. All soldiers were given passes to go into town. Since white men could not exist for long in the bush, the military authorities did not worry much about their getting away. Some of the natives might help deserters, but others, in return for large rewards, would hunt them down. Then, too, owners or captains of British ships in port, as short of hands as they might be, would hesitate to sign on men that they suspected might be deserters from the garrison. With all this in mind, Ebenezer and his friends decided to try to make their way overland to the north coast. There, they hoped to get a small boat by hook or by crook, in which they could sail to Cuba, just across Montego Bay. In clear weather, one could look from Jamaica right across to the mountain peaks in Cuba.

Since Spain had become an ally of France in support of the American colonists, there was a good chance of finding American privateers or merchantmen in a Cuban port.

Two of the plotters who worked in the armory stole three swords and a pair of pistols. These weapons together with clothes and food were hidden in a hut. On the day set for their escape, Ebenezer asked for evening passes to town for himself and his friends, a favor which the commanding officer was pleased to grant his favorite barber.

The supplies and weapons were taken from the hut. But, fearing that six soldiers carrying bundles would look suspicious, the men separated, naming a

62

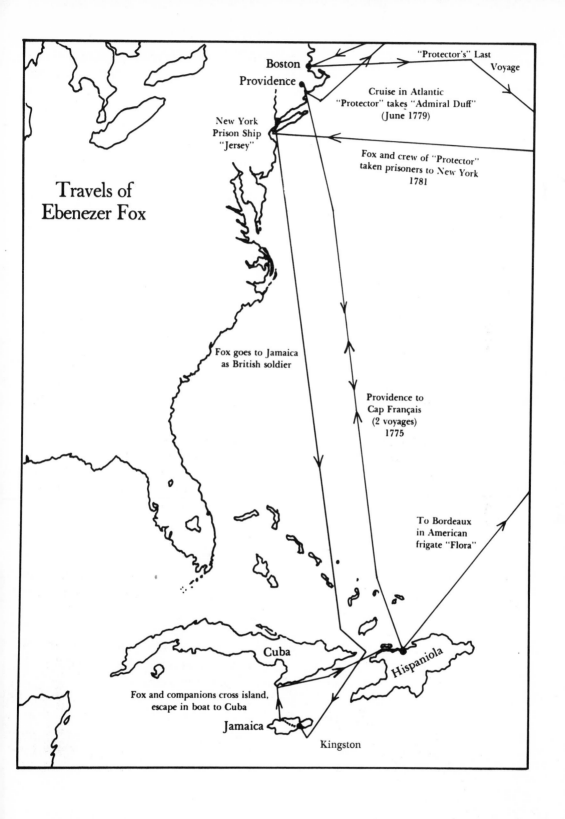

Travels of
Ebenezer Fox

Boston
Providence

New York
Prison Ship
"Jersey"

"Protector's" Last
Voyage

Cruise in Atlantic
"Protector" takes "Admiral Duff"
(June 1779)

Fox and crew of "Protector"
taken prisoners to New York
1781

Fox goes to Jamaica
as British soldier

Providence to
Cap Français
(2 voyages)
1775

To Bordeaux
in American
frigate "Flora"

Cuba

Hispaniola

Fox and companions cross island,
escape in boat to Cuba

Jamaica

Kingston

place where they would meet later. One man failed to show up and the fugitives never did learn what happened to him. Ebenezer and the four other conspirators changed out of their uniforms, armed themselves, and pushed inland northward as fast as possible.

A chance meeting with a slightly tipsy British sergeant gave them a bad turn. Mistaking them for new recruits for a nearby regiment, he kept insisting on accompanying them to their barracks. It became obvious to the five deserters that in order to save their own lives, their friendly guide would have to lose his. Then, just in the nick of time, the sergeant remembered that his own pass to town would expire within a short while, and he hurried off to Kingston, never knowing how close to death he had come.

In the beginning, the companions traveled at night, hiding in the dense jungle growth during the day. After three days, their provisions were gone and they decided to risk traveling by day.

They had not been on the road long before three Negroes armed with muskets suddenly appeared and ordered them to halt.

The deserters had discovered earlier that the pistols were useless, and they kept their swords concealed under their clothes. Tired and hungry, they were no match for three stout men with muskets. Their only hope was to bluff their way out. Suspecting that their captors could not read, one of the Americans named Jones took an old letter from his pocket. Holding it up, he called out to the Negroes that he had a pass for the party to cross the island. At the same time, he and the others kept walking nonchalantly toward the leveled muskets.

Ebenezer wrote: "We advanced steadily forward, shoulder to shoulder, till the breast of three of us were within a few inches of the muzzles of their guns. Jones reached forward and handed the paper to one of the Negroes. He took it and, having turned it round several times and examined both sides, and finding himself not much the wiser for it,

Brass Navy Pistol with Spring Bayonet

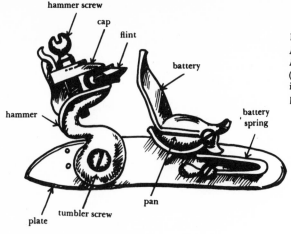

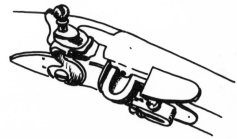

FLINTLOCK
Left: exterior parts of lock.
Below: hammer partway back
(half cock) and battery forward
in loading position. Powder was
poured in pan and battery closed.

Left: When hammer was pulled all
the way back to full cock and the
trigger squeezed, hammer flew forward
and flint struck battery, knocking it open.
Sparks ignited exposed powder and flash traveled
through touch-hole to charge in gun.

shook his head and said, 'We must stop you.' The expression on his countenance, the doubts which were manifested in his manner of receiving the paper, convinced us that all hope of deceiving or conciliating them was at an end.

"Their muskets were still presented, their fingers upon the triggers. An awful pause of a moment ensued. Then we made a sudden and desperate spring forward and seized their muskets. Our attack was so unexpected that we wrenched the weapons from their hands before they were aware of

our intention. The Negro whom I attacked fired just as I seized his gun. Fortunately, I had turned the direction of it and the ball inflicted a slight wound upon my side, the scar of which remains to this day. This was the only gun that was discharged during this dreadful encounter."

"As soon as it was in my possession," Ebenezer continued in his account of his experiences, "I exercised all my strength, more than I thought I possessed, and gave him a tremendous blow over the head with the breech. The blow brought him to the ground, from which he never rose."

The other two Negroes were felled just as quickly. The whole affair was over in a few seconds. Half a minute later, the bodies had been dragged into the underbrush and the dusty road was empty. The men took their victims' food and ammunition and added the one serviceable musket to their arsenal.

After that, the party avoided the roads altogether, hiking across the heavily wooded mountain range which runs down the center of the island. One more night's journey brought them to within sight of the coast.

"I doubt," wrote Ebenezer, "whether Columbus and his crew experienced more heartfelt joy when they saw the new world than our little party did when we discovered the sea."

To the north, they could dimly see the island of Cuba, but to reach it they had to have a boat. It is said that fortune favors the brave, and before sunset they spied a small craft beating in against an offshore wind. Quickly concealing themselves near the water's edge, not far from several native huts, the five men waited with their one musket carefully primed and loaded. At last the right moment came. Bang! went the musket; down dropped the man at the helm and the boat surged toward the beach. In an instant the Americans scrambled aboard, and steered the craft out to sea.

The noise of the shot brought a crowd of Negroes from the huts. They at once opened fire on the fugitives, but the shots went wide and the boat was soon out of range.

There were three men and a boy in the crew—the steersman had merely been grazed by the ball. The Americans ordered them overboard and they all dived into the water and swam back to shore.

The crowd of people on the beach were determined to catch the men who had seized the boat. Some of them boarded a schooner, anchored close by, and gave chase. But night was falling. By frequent changes of course, the Americans were able to elude their pursuers in the growing darkness.

At dawn, they found themselves near the Cuban shore, with the schooner not far away. A chase followed. The schooner's crew banged away with a swivel gun while the Americans replied as best they could with their single musket. As the Americans neared the shore of Cuba, their pursuers were forced to give up the chase. Ebenezer and his companions were greeted by friendly Cubans who took them in a small coaster to Cap Français. There, to their joy, they found the American frigate "Flora."

The frigate was bound for France. Ebenezer's companions wanted a direct passage home, so the little band broke up. Ebenezer, his appetite for adventure not yet satisfied, joined the "Flora's" crew. But he was not to set sail without one more alarming experience.

While ashore, he and some friends were seized by a French press-gang and hurried on board a French warship at anchor in the harbor. In those days, captains often sent out detachments of men under an officer to forcibly round up enough seamen to make a full crew.

Typical 36-Gun Frigate of the Revolutionary War Period

1. Jib
2. Fore Topmast Staysail
3. Fore Staysail
4. Main Topgallant Staysail
5. Middle Staysail
6. Main Topmast Staysail
7. Main Staysail

8. Mizzen Topgallant Staysail
9. Mizzen Topmast Staysail
10. Mizzen Staysail
11. Mizzen
12. Spritsail Topsail
13. Spritsail Course
14. Fore Topgallant Sail

15. Fore Topsail
16. Fore Course
17. Main Topgallant Sail
18. Main Topsail
19. Main Course
20. Mizzen Topgallant Sail
21. Mizzen Topsail

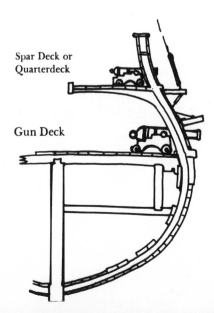

Spar Deck or
Quarterdeck

Gun Deck

Thirty-six-gun frigates carried their main armament, usually 18-pounders, on one deck. Smaller guns, often 9-pounders, were usually carried on the quarterdeck or spar deck. Cross section at left shows arrangements. Notice the way the sides curve inward ("tumble home") to help keep the weight of the cannon near the center line.

All seamen, and many a landlubber as well, were considered fair game. Ebenezer and his friends protested fruitlessly that they were Americans and members of the crew of the "Flora." The French captain was short of men and refused to release them.

Ebenezer kept his own counsel and that night when he saw his chance, he slipped over the side. Braving the sharks which infested those waters, he swam to the "Flora." Next day, the American captain demanded the return of his men and they were sent back with the French captain's apologies for the "mistake."

The "Flora" made a successful voyage, capturing a couple of prizes, on her way to Bordeaux. The British blockade was so effective, however, that no ships could get out and the "Flora" was laid up, awaiting further orders from America. She was still waiting when peace was signed in the spring of 1783, and so Ebenezer saw no further action.

He returned to America and his job in the barber shop. At twenty-one, when his apprentice days were over, Ebenezer Fox went into business for himself. Whatever his skill with razor and curling irons, it is certain that his customers never lacked for tales of high adventure.

JOSEPH MARTIN
Sees the War Through

JOHN GREENWOOD AND EBENEZER FOX were typical young Americans of the Revolution. They enlisted in the Army or went to sea and did their duty. That duty done, they returned to civilian life. The story of Joseph Martin, however, is that of a boy who decided, after a short-term enlistment, to see the war through in the Continental Army. This he did, serving until June, 1783.

His military life was like that of most Continental soldiers, with periods of sharp fighting, long marches, and even longer periods of boredom. He was often wet, and often bitterly cold and always hungry, sometimes almost to the point of starvation.

Joseph was born in 1760 in Becket, Massachusetts. At the age of seven, he went to live with his grandparents. As a farm boy, he was used to hard work and a rigorous life. Undoubtedly, his early years on the farm helped him to survive the hardships of years of service in the Continental Army. He apparently received little, if any, formal schooling. Nevertheless, the account that he wrote of his adventures is literate and contains flashes of humor which lead the reader to believe that no matter how rough the going, Joseph could usually see the bright side of things.

He was excited, as were many boys, by the stirring happenings of 1775, but he was under legal age for regular service. In June, 1776, he enlisted for six months in the Massachusetts troops, wishing "only to take a priming before I took upon me the whole coat of paint of a soldier," as he put it. The troops were to be sent to bolster the colonists' defenses of New York, which Sir William Howe was threatening with a large British force.

The war actually began for Joseph on August 27, when the men of his regiment were each given a couple of handfuls of sea bread "nearly hard enough for musket flints" and ferried across the East River to the Long Island shore.

The din of heavy firing ahead told them that Washington's men were engaged with the enemy. They pushed on, "marching to the sound of the guns," although the Battle of Long Island had already gone against the Colonials. The Massachusetts regiment arrived at Gowanus Creek just in time to see the Delaware and Maryland regiments driven into the muddy waters by the advancing British. The fire of the men of Massa-chusetts checked the victorious redcoats and saved many of the routed Colonials.

Next day, there was much firing near the creek but no hand-to-hand fighting. The redcoats had learned to respect the musketfire of the Americans. On the other hand, the Americans had found that they were no match for the British regulars with the bayonet.

On the following night, Joseph's regiment was ordered to return as quietly as

possible to the ferry and go back to Manhattan Island.

Here they were engaged in strengthening the fortifications of the city, and daybreak of September 15 saw Joseph and his comrades entrenched on the shore of Kip's Bay at the end of present-day Thirty-fourth Street. As the light increased they could see British warships anchored within musket shot and, when the flatboats carrying the redcoats

crept out from the Long Island shore, so many that they appeared "like a large clover field in bloom," these vessels opened fire.

• "There came such a peal of thunder from the British shipping that I thought my head would go with the sound. I made a frog's leap for the ditch and began to consider which part of my carcass would go first." The American lines consisted only of a shallow trench with the earth thrown toward the enemy. These flimsy earthworks were held until they were all but leveled by the close-range fire of some seventy cannon. Then the order was given to retreat. Behind the earthworks was a piece of open ground swept by the British guns. Joseph and his comrades dashed across this, while cannon balls and grapeshot whistled by their ears.

The panic-stricken militia fled, with the British infantry hard on their heels. It was only Howe's failure to advance right across the island to the North River that allowed any of the city's defenders to escape. By the next day the scattered Americans had regrouped at Harlem Heights. Here they drove the advancing British back. This engagement, in which Joseph counted nineteen bullet holes in one rail of a fence near where he was stationed, helped the Americans regain some of the confidence they had lost in the rout of the day before.

A lull in operations followed the bat-

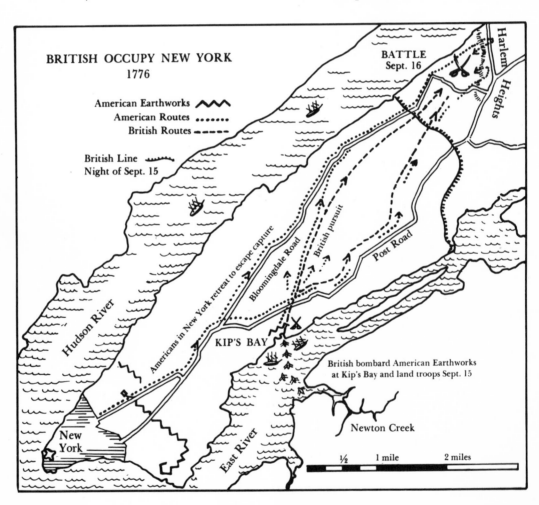

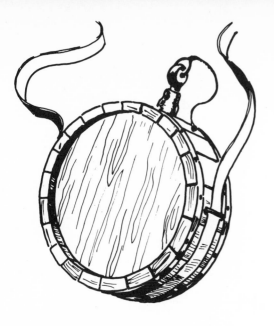

Wooden Canteen

tle in Harlem Heights. In the cold, wet
weather of early October, Joseph and
his companions had occasion to regret
the loss of their spare clothing and blan-
kets in the hasty retreat from Kip's Bay.

"To have to lie on the cold and often
wet ground without a blanket and with
nothing but thin summer clothing was
tedious," reported Joseph, in one of his
typical understatements. Also, he was
beginning to notice the scarcity of food,
a lack that was to plague the American
armies all through the war.

Joseph recalled a man complaining of
hunger after the action at Harlem
Heights, when none of the troops had
eaten for forty-eight hours. He wrote,
"The colonel, putting his hand in his
pocket, took out a piece of an ear of
Indian corn burnt as black as coal.
'Here,' he said to the complaining man,
'eat this and learn to be a soldier.' "

One of Washington's commanders
was the fiery and bad-tempered General
Israel Putnam. Young Martin told of
being about to crawl through a rail fence
one day when the old officer galloped
toward him and ordered him to let
down the bars.

Joseph related how, with the independence typical of a fifteen-year-old,
he "slipped through, leaving him to let
down the bars himself. He was apparently in a dreadful passion. Drawing a
pistol from his holster, he came after me
to the bars, with his usual exclamation,
'Curse ye!' "

But Joseph was by then safe in a
thicket, laughing at the way a private
had gotten the best of a general.

When the British under General William Howe marched to New Rochelle,

Flintlock Pistol

The action centered mainly around Chatterton's Hill on the American right. A combined attack of British and Germans, although supported by heavy artillery fire, met with resolute resistance. Then a charge of British cavalry, kettle-drums beating and trumpets sounding, threw the militia regiments into a panic. The green troops fled, and scores were cut down or captured. This threw the American right wing into confusion. But, thanks to the steadiness of the Delaware regiment, a general retreat was made in fairly good order.

Joseph's regiment was in the midst of the battle and suffered many casualties. Joseph remembered particularly a hot fight in an orchard, with bullets flying through the branches, and bodies, some in red coats and some in blue, huddled among the fruit trees.

KETTLE DRUMS and DRUM BANNER

BRITISH DRAGOON, TROOPER

gathered up the Hessian reinforcements, and started out cross-country for White Plains, New York, Washington concentrated his troops near the town on the crest of some hills between the Bronx River on the east and a lake on the west.

74

CAVALRY TRUMPET and

TRUMPET BANNER

ships. After several sharp skirmishes, however, the British were able to reach their vessels and embarked for New York.

Washington had rightly said that smallpox was more to be dreaded than the sword of the enemy, and was determined that all his soldiers be inoculated. Inoculation in those days should

Hunger and exposure had weakened many of Washington's men. Many more gave up and went home. Joseph stayed with his regiment, but he was in poor physical condition and took no part in the fighting at Fort Washington and in New Jersey. He was discharged on Christmas Day and started back to Massachusetts, having learned enough of a soldier's life, he declared, to keep him home for the future.

Yet spring found Joseph, now sixteen, ready to go to war once more. On April 12, 1777, he re-enlisted for the duration in the Eighth Connecticut Regiment of Continentals. Later that spring, British troops landed in Connecticut and burned the town of Danbury, with its large store of military supplies. The newly enlisted men and the militia attempted to cut off the raiders from their

AMERICAN INFANTRYMAN – CONTINENTAL LINE

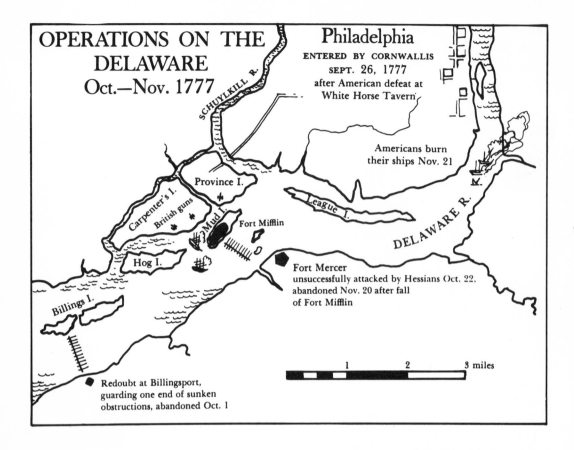

OPERATIONS ON THE
DELAWARE
Oct.—Nov. 1777

SCHUYLKILL R.

Philadelphia

ENTERED BY CORNWALLIS
SEPT. 26, 1777
after American defeat at
White Horse Tavern

Americans burn
their ships Nov. 21

Province I.

Carpenter's I.

British guns

Mud I.

Fort Mifflin

League I.

DELAWARE R.

Hog I.

Fort Mercer
unsuccessfully attacked by Hessians Oct. 22,
abandoned Nov. 20 after fall
of Fort Mifflin

Billings I.

1   2   3 miles

Redoubt at Billingsport,
guarding one end of sunken
obstructions, abandoned Oct. 1

not be confused with today's vaccination against smallpox, polio and other diseases. In Colonial times it consisted of being given a mild case of the disease, which commonly caused only a few pocks and was seldom fatal, whereas the natural disease carried a high fatality rate, and usually those victims who escaped death were disfigured. However, inoculation was dreaded, not without reason, and it must have been with some reluctance that Joseph and his companions were marched off to barracks to receive the infection.

After recovering, Joseph's company was detached for advance guard duty near New York. Speaking of this service, he wrote: "The whole time is spent in marches, especially night marches, watching, starving, and in cold weather, freezing and sickness. If they get any chance to rest, it must be in the woods or fields, under the side of a fence, in an orchard or in any other place but for a comfortable one, lying on the cold and often wet ground, and perhaps, before the eyes can be closed with a moment's sleep, alarmed and compelled to stand under arms an hour or two, or to receive an attack from the enemy."

76

When this duty was over, the company rejoined the regiment at Peekskill, New York, and shortly afterward marched to join the main army in Pennsylvania. Joseph did not have much to say about the defeat at Germantown. His brigade advanced, drove the enemy through their camp and, then, in their turn, were forced to retreat. He thought that lack of ammunition had much to do with the defeat. It was reported that, when Washington tried to rally the fleeing troops, they held out empty cartridge boxes to show him why they ran. After marching some twenty miles into battle and fighting for nearly three hours, the exhausted troops retreated for twenty-four miles, having had no food on either leg of their journey.

There followed some marching and countermarching around Barren Hill. To Joseph's disgust, they had to ford the Schuylkill River several times in water waist-deep, in weather so cold that their wet clothes froze. All he could find to eat on this expedition were a few walnuts.

The Eighth and the Fourth Connecticut regiments were next ordered to the forts on the Delaware River. These had been erected to keep the British from reaching Philadelphia by water. A key position was Fort Mifflin, a rambling structure, part stone, part earthwork, part wooden palisade, built on Mud Island. It mounted only a few guns and was garrisoned by about 450 men. Against it, the British brought

TYPICAL EARTHWORKS — Troops who forced their way through the abatis were exposed to fire from cannon in the embrasures and musketry from the parapet which swept the long slope of the glacis. The ditch and the exterior slope were deep enough to require the use of scaling ladders. Projecting works (bastions) were laid out so that fire from them swept the ditch from end to end. Meanwhile, shells, grenades and flaming tar barrels were rolled down into the men struggling to climb the scarp. The berm was to keep debris knocked from the parapet from filling the ditch.

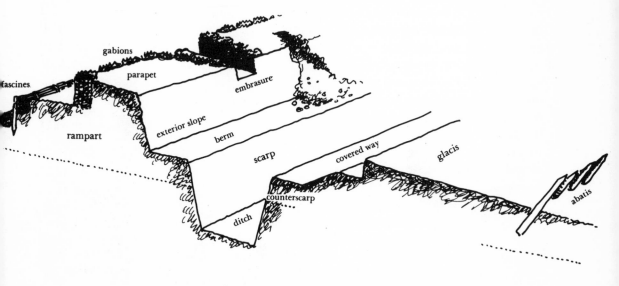

warships, a floating battery, heavy siege guns and mortars.

For five days the bombardment went on until all but two of the fort's guns were dismounted, much damage done to the works, and many of the garrison killed and wounded.

Besides keeping up a fire from their few remaining cannon at night, the men attempted to repair the damage done to the works during the day.

"During the whole night at intervals of a quarter or half an hour, the enemy would let off all their pieces. We had sentinels to watch them and at every flash of their guns to cry, 'A shot!' Upon hearing this, everyone endeavored to take care of himself, yet they would ever and anon, in spite of all our precautions, cut up some of us."

There was no shot for the one heavy gun, a thirty-two-pounder, in the fort.

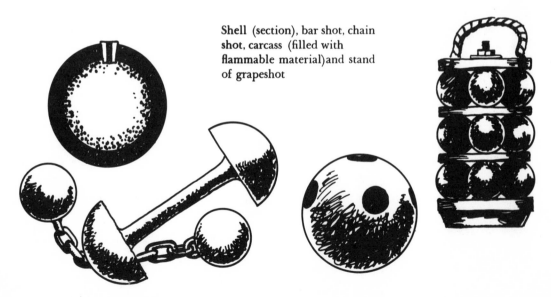

Shell (section), bar shot, chain shot, carcass (filled with flammable material) and stand of grapeshot

So, a reward of a gill of rum was offered for shot of that caliber from the British batteries. Joseph often saw, he said, "From twenty to fifty of our men standing on the parade, waiting with impatience the coming of the shot. It would often be seized before its motion had fully ceased and conveyed off to our gun to be sent back again to its former owners."

On November 15, warships mounting over 240 guns joined in the attack. The effect was devastating. An estimated one thousand shots were fired every twenty minutes. Joseph saw five of the crew at a gun cut down with one ball. "The whole area of the fort was as completely ploughed as a field," he said. "The buildings of every kind were hanging in broken fragments and the guns were all dismounted."

The battered fort was held until nightfall. Then the dead and the wounded were ferried across the river and the

ruins set on fire. Joseph was in one of the last boats to leave. He remembered that the British saw them in the glare from the burning buildings.

"Almost their whole fire was directed at us," he wrote afterwards. "Sometimes our boat seemed to be almost thrown out of the water. At length a shot took the sternpost out of the rear boat. We had then to stop and take the men from the crippled boat into the other two. Now the shot and water flew merrily, but, by the assistance of a kind Providence, we escaped without any further injury and landed, a little after midnight, on the Jersey shore."

Joseph recorded no further action that winter. In fact, all his energy and that of the rest of the men seemed to have been devoted to finding enough food to stay alive. By a stroke of luck, young Martin was detailed to a foraging party and spent much of that terrible winter in the rich Pennsylvania-Dutch farming country. Their job was to requisition food supplies for the wagon trains to transport to the army. Naturally, Joseph and his squad managed to live well and wax fat while their comrades at Valley Forge were half-starved.

But one day orders came for the detail to return to camp. Before long, Joseph, now seventeen, was busy learning the Prussian method of drilling from Baron Friedrich von Steuben. This German officer came to help General Washington by drilling the bands of American country men and reorganizing them into a unified and effective fighting force. General Steuben never returned to Germany. He dropped his title, became an American citizen, and bought a house and farm on land that is today East Fifty-second Street in New York City.

Some Positions from a Manual of Exercises of the Revolutionary War Period

Fix bayonet.

Right: rest your finelock.

Charge bayonet.

Take aim. Fire!

Right: ram down cartridge.

When the British left Philadelphia and marched through New Jersey on their way to New York, the Continental Army followed them. On June 28, 1778, the Battle of Monmouth was fought. Here, for the first time, the value of Steuben's painstaking drilling was seen, for the Continentals behaved like veteran soldiers, marching and wheeling into position under fire as if they were on parade.

The day was almost lost, however, when General Charles Lee ordered a retirement of his division at a critical stage of the battle. Washington's anger and his rage at Lee were remembered ever afterwards by those who witnessed the scene. Joseph was close enough to Washington to hear him ask by whose orders the troops were retreating, and he observed that the usually calm Commander-in-Chief seemed "to be in a great passion." It took all the energy of the general and his staff to halt the retreat. After heavy fighting, the British were brought to a standstill. That night they quietly retreated, leaving the field to the Americans.

The army proceeded to White Plains via King's Ferry and Tarrytown. While there, Joseph was transferred to the

American Light Infantryman

newly formed Light Infantry Corps. One company of each regiment of the army was designated a Light Company which was made up of young men who were good marksmen and physically tough. These companies were then formed into a separate corps for special duties. Joseph found the service with these eighteenth-century commandos even harder than that with the regular line.

Light Infantry Cap

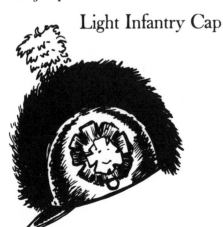

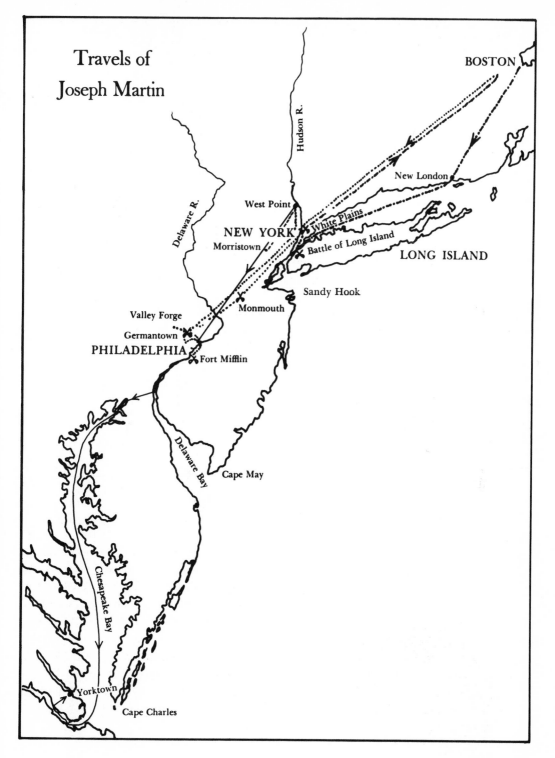

Travels of
Joseph Martin

BOSTON

Hudson R.

Delaware R.

West Point

New London

NEW YORK

White Plains

Morristown

Battle of Long Island

LONG ISLAND

Sandy Hook

Valley Forge

Monmouth

Germantown

PHILADELPHIA

Fort Mifflin

Delaware Bay

Cape May

Chesapeake Bay

Yorktown

Cape Charles

Broadaxe, and Froe (used for splitting blocks for shingles).

By the winter of 1778, he was back with his regiment—"in our Continental line of starving and freezing." Conditions were so bad that there were several minor mutinies. Joseph's regiment paraded without orders to demand better treatment. The officers, who were little, if any, better off than the men, "with an abundance of fair promises, persuaded us to return to our quarters again," said Joseph. Too hungry to sleep, the troops decided that the officers should not sleep either, and there was a constant banging of muskets throughout the night.

There was little anyone could do. Supplies were practically unobtainable. The Continental paper money with which the soldiers were paid, was as Joseph put it, "worth about as much as its weight in rags." Furloughs were freely granted and Joseph spent some time with his grandparents.

Duties for the Eighth Connecticut in 1779 were fairly light. There were no pitched battles, although there was a great deal of marching and skirmishing, most of it on short rations and sometimes in bare feet.

The winter at Valley Forge in 1777-78 has become famous in American history, but it could not match in severity the winter of 1779-80, the coldest of the eighteenth century. After a miserable march from Peekskill, New York, to Morristown, New Jersey, in bitter cold and deep snow, the worn-out soldiers set to work to build their winter quarters.

The timber for the rough huts had to be felled and cut to size. Then the ends were notched and the logs laid up in regular log-cabin style. The chinks were stuffed with moss or plastered with clay. The roofs were made up of rough shingles, split out of short lengths of log. A chimney of stones set in clay was built at the end of each hut. Wooden bunks with evergreen boughs for mattresses and short chunks of logs for stools completed the huts, which were about twelve feet by fifteen feet and housed several men.

Kept on less than half-rations and without receiving any pay for months, it is not surprising that by spring the army had dwindled to fewer than 4,000 men fit for duty. On May 25, the regiments of the Connecticut Line mutinied. There seems to have been open insubordination, but no violence, nor were any punishments meted out. The troops, although they were still discontented, remained with the army.

Joseph wrote afterward, "Our stir did us some good in the end, for we had provisions directly after, so we had no great cause for complaint for some time."

TYPICAL LOG HUT, Showing Method of
Construction. Logs on shingles *(below)* were
to keep them in place.

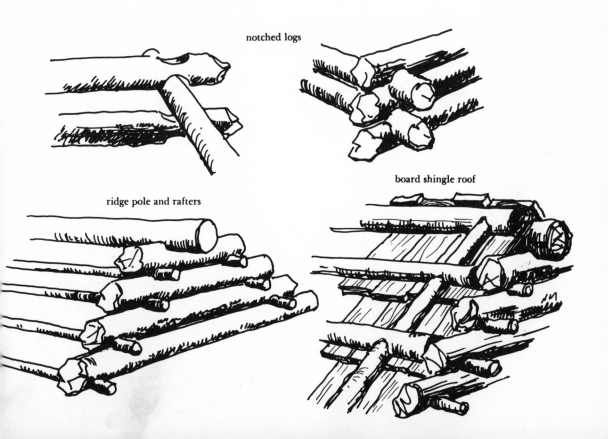

notched logs

board shingle roof

ridge pole and rafters

In the summer of 1780, he was chosen to be one of the newly formed Corps of Sappers and Miners, and promoted to sergeant. Joseph soon found, however, that his higher rank was not accompanied by an increase in rations. Sergeant Martin was just as hungry as Private Martin.

He spent the summer and fall building fortifications and, occasionally, he took part in a skirmish with the local Tories.

During the winter of 1780-81, Joseph was in barracks at West Point, about which he made no comment in his account of his wartime experiences. Presumably that winter was passed a little more comfortably than the previous one. With spring, fighting began again, mainly skirmishes with the Tories. Joseph had several narrow escapes and in one ambush by Cowboys, as the Tories were sometimes called, he nearly lost his life.

This happened when a small scouting party of which he had charge was surprised and nearly surrounded. A hasty retreat was made and Sergeant Martin found himself last, with the enemy close

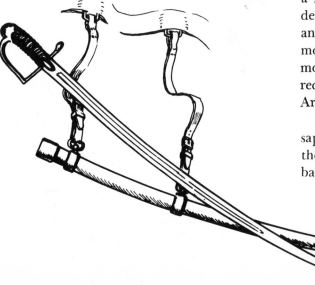

behind him. A fence blocked his escape and, in trying to scramble over it, he somehow got hung up, with one foot caught in the crotch of a tree whose low boughs brushed against the fence.

The enemy commander gave him a deep cut in the leg with his sword. But, before the man could strike again, Joseph wriggled free. As he fell on the other side of the fence, he got a good look at his attacker and was startled to recognize an old friend.

"When we were boys, he was one of my most familiar playmates," Joseph said. "And he was with me as a messmate in the campaign of 1776. He had enlisted during the war in 1777, but sometime before this, had deserted to the enemy."

So by a queer twist of fate, Joseph received his only wound of the war at the hands of an old friend.

In August the combined American and French forces began their march to Yorktown, Virginia. As the army's experts on siege warfare, the one hundred and ten men of the Corps of Sappers and Miners were among the first to set out. From Philadelphia, Joseph's party sailed down the Delaware in a schooner full of gunpowder, a cargo which made them a little nervous during a violent thunderstorm. Before leaving the city, Joseph and his fellow sappers had received a month's pay, not in script but in hard money, the first (and last) that Joseph received while he was in the Continental Army.

From the mouth of the Delaware, the sappers went overland to the head of the Chesapeake Bay, where they embarked for the James River.

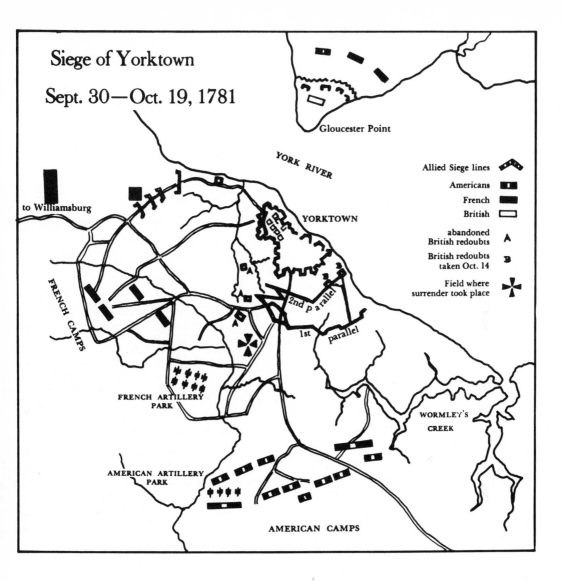

Siege of Yorktown
Sept. 30—Oct. 19, 1781

Gloucester Point

YORK RIVER

YORKTOWN

to Williamsburg

FRENCH CAMPS

2nd parallel

1st parallel

FRENCH ARTILLERY
PARK

WORMLEY'S
CREEK

AMERICAN ARTILLERY
PARK

AMERICAN CAMPS

Allied Siege lines
Americans
French
British

abandoned
British redoubts   A

British redoubts
taken Oct. 14   B

Field where
surrender took place

The position of Cornwallis at Yorktown at this time was almost hopeless. Command of the sea had been temporarily lost and the French fleet under Comte de Grasse blockaded the mouth of the York River. The British had fewer than 6,000 combat troops, many of whom were sick. They were faced by French-American armies with more than 16,000 men. In New York, however, General Henry Clinton had 7,000 men ready to go to the aid of Cornwallis, and the British fleet, with new reinforcements, was almost ready to sail. Therefore, the Americans had to press the siege as rapidly as possible, and the lines for the first trenches were laid out on the night of October 5.

While Joseph's sappers were helping the engineer officers, who were in charge of the work a few hundred yards from the British defenses, a senior officer, not one of their corps, suddenly appeared. He questioned Joseph and his men and conferred with the officers. It was not until Joseph heard the man addressed as "Excellency" that he realized that the midnight visitor was General Washington.

The trenches were laid out. On the following night, Washington himself struck a few symbolic blows with a pick-axe before the waiting parties of men set to work with their entrenching tools. The Americans always surprised the British by their skill and industry with pick and shovel. It was not many days before French and American siege guns were blazing away at the British defense works and redoubts, and a second line of trenches was begun.

Before they could be completed, however, two strong redoubts had to be captured. Preparations were made for the assault. To the Sappers and Miners was given the task of cutting through the abatis, formed by felled trees with sharpened branches placed in front of the British trenches. In those days, the abatis took the place of modern barbed wire entanglements. Armed with axes, Joseph and his comrades were to go ahead, to chop a passage for the attacking soldiers.

In describing the action later, Joseph wrote: "At dark the detachment was formed and advanced beyond the trenches and lay down on the ground to await the signal for advancing to the attack. That signal was to be three shells

from a certain battery near where we were lying. All the batteries in our line were silent, and we lay anxiously waiting for the signal."

Everyone was tense, for any second the British trenches might erupt in spurts of flame and flying lead. The storming party hugged the ground, axes and muskets gripped in sweaty hands. Of a sudden, a series of three loud ex-

plosions broke the stillness, and fiery trails of shells soared upward in the darkness. As one man, American and French attackers got up and moved quickly and quietly toward the British redoubts. Still, the British lines were silent. Then, as the first of the stormers reached the abatis, the flashes of musket-fire lit up the British entrenchments.

With savage yells, the attackers swarmed forward as Joseph and his sappers swung their axes in frantic haste to clear the way for them. Bullets and grapeshot flew everywhere and men began to drop. But the axes slashed and chopped and the way was clear at last. With fixed bayonets, the stormers charged through the gap and leaped the embankment into the first redoubt, or small fort.

89

The Sappers and Miners had been forbidden to enter the fort. But in their eagerness to get at the enemy, they forgot their orders. The enemy were throwing small shells with their fuses lit into the trench. As Joseph crossed it, the flashes from the explosions and the glare of musketry were so bright that he could recognize the faces of his comrades.

Although the small British force fought bravely, it was soon overpowered. The other small fort was taken. And the victorious troops set to work at once to secure the captured works against any counterattack. They need not have troubled themselves, as it happened. The British lines had been badly weakened by the loss of the two strongholds, and too few men remained to attempt a counteroffensive.

On the night of October 16, Cornwallis made a last desperate attempt to evacuate the British troops from Yorktown by ferrying them across the York River. Just as he was about to start across, a storm, with gale winds and heavy rain, drove him back.

GABION, Showing Method of Construction (it was then filled with earth) and Chevaux--de-frise

At dawn on Wednesday, Washington began a furious cannonading of the Yorktown lines. That day marked the end for Cornwallis and his army. He called for an armistice to discuss terms, but Washington demanded complete surrender.

On the seventeenth, General Cornwallis wrote: "Sir, I propose a cessation of hostilities for twenty-four hours, and that two officers may be appointed by each side, to meet at Mr. Moore's house [a nearby farmhouse] to settle terms for the surrender of the posts at York and Gloucester." This was the document for which Washington and the men of his army like Joseph Martin had fought for so long.

On October 19, the ceremony of the surrender took place. The defeated British troops marched between the lines of the Continental Army and the militia and the French troops, and laid down their arms.

"It was a noble sight to us," wrote Joseph, "and the more so, as it seemed to promise a speedy conclusion to the contest."

And so it proved. Although it was not until September 3, 1783, that the formal treaty, which acknowledged the independence of the United States, was signed, hostilities practically ceased. Until peace was officially declared, however, Joseph was still in the army. With the other sappers, he was engaged in several projects. In the spring of '82 an attack of yellow fever struck him down and almost accomplished what the bullets and bayonets of the enemy had failed to do. Many of Joseph's comrades died of that dreaded scourge, a sorry ending

French Infantryman
Regiment Soissonais

Hussar
Regiment Lauzun

for men who had fought a long war and for whom peace and a return to civil life was in sight.

It was not until June, 1783, that Joseph was finally discharged. It would be pleasant to be able to tell that a grateful Congress made up at the finish for the years of starvation and lack of pay with a handsome bonus. But old services were already forgotten, and the insecure and thrifty politicians—after cutting the Continental Army down to eighty men and a few officers—refused even three months' back pay. And so Joseph and his fellow soldiers trudged home—many of them selling their muskets to pay their way—bitter, no doubt, but knowing that their courage and resolution had finally won victory.

BULLET MOLD, with Sprue Cutter Lead Ladle and Bullet with Tail or Sprue

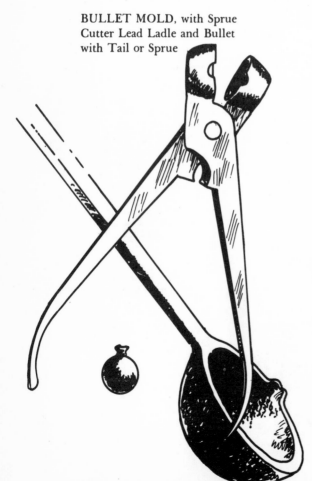

Paper Cartridges. Ball, and "Buck and Ball" (one musket ball and three buckshot).

John Greenwood, Ebenezer Fox and Joseph Martin—three boys who served their country well. In the wilds of Canada, on the high seas and through the hard-fought battles and terrible winters of Washington's campaigns, these youngsters showed that they could do everything that grown men could do. And there were many like them, some of them even younger than John, Ebenezer and Joseph. Moved by patriotism and a true American spirit of adventure, they faced danger and hardship, and helped found a free nation. Without them and those like them, the Revolution would have been lost. They fought for liberty, their own and that of the generations to come after them.

Early in 1783, the French ship "Triomphe" entered Delaware Bay and went up the river, with bells clanging and sailors shouting, to Philadelphia. She brought the news that Great Britain had signed a treaty of peace in Paris in November. This was a preliminary treaty. All hostilities ceased. The United States of America was a new, free and independent nation, recognized by the British Crown.

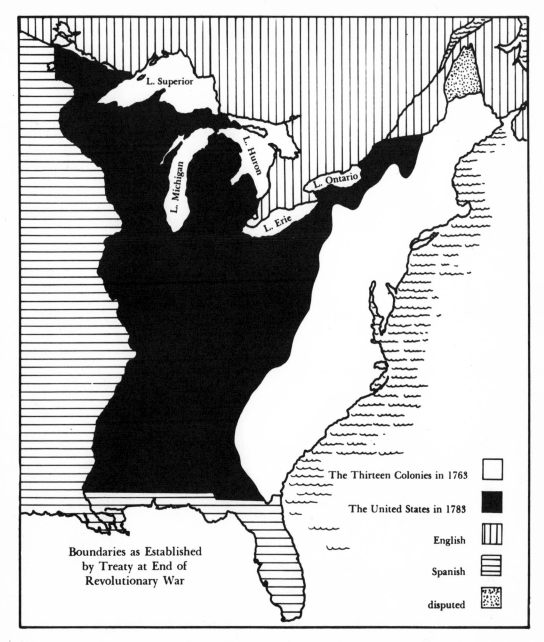

L. Superior

L. Michigan

L. Huron

L. Ontario

L. Erie

The Thirteen Colonies in 1763

The United States in 1783

English

Spanish

disputed

Boundaries as Established
by Treaty at End of
Revolutionary War

In the final Treaty of Paris, signed on September 3, 1783, Great Britain granted all the territory south to Florida, north to Canada, and west to the forts in the Ohio Valley, which included the present states of Michigan, Illinois, Ohio, Indiana and Wisconsin, to the new nation. To France went the tiny island of Tobago, and to Spain, the Floridas and Minorca.

At Newburgh, New York, on April 19, 1783, the eighth anniversary of the Battle of Lexington, General George Washington held simple ceremonies symbolizing the end of the long war for the Continental Army. In his speech, Washington declared that "happy, thrice happy, shall they be pronounced hereafter, who have contributed anything, who have performed the meanest office, in erecting this stupendous fabric of freedom and empire on the broad basis of independency; who have assisted in protecting the rights of human nature, and establishing an asylum for the poor and oppressed of all nations and religions." These words were meant for boys, now men, like John Greenwood, Ebenezer Fox, and Joseph Martin, as well as those who listened to their Commander-in-Chief that day under the trees beside the Hudson River.

The future of the new nation was made by boys as well as by men.

GUIDE TO

What's in the Illustrations